THOMAS WOTTON'S
LETTER-BOOK
1574–1586

WEST FRONT OF BOUGHTON PLACE

The small doorway at the south end belongs to the early fifteenth century, the square-headed
windows above are a century later. All beyond the change of pitch in the roof is the work
of 1560, except the northern end, which is of brick, and possibly of 1584

THOMAS WOTTON'S
LETTER-BOOK
1574–1586

EDITED BY

G. ELAND, F.S.A.

LONDON
OXFORD UNIVERSITY PRESS
NEW YORK   TORONTO
1960

Oxford University Press, Amen House, London E.C.4

GLASGOW NEW YORK TORONTO MELBOURNE WELLINGTON
BOMBAY CALCUTTA MADRAS KARACHI KUALA LUMPUR
CAPE TOWN IBADAN NAIROBI ACCRA

PRINTED IN GREAT BRITAIN

The following pages are inscribed to
MR. & MRS. DAVID J. CLARK
as a slight recognition of the
care and sympathy with which they are
preserving all that is left of
the house in which most of the letters
which follow were written

INTRODUCTION

THE writer of the letters here printed for the first time needs no introduction to lovers of our literature. Izaak Walton gives a very fair account of Thomas Wotton in the life of his youngest son which he prefixed to *Reliquiae Wottonianae* in 1657, and since then it has been included in all editions of 'Walton's Lives'.

Izaak was not born until six years after Thomas had died, so that his information about the father must have come from the son, and Sir Henry was only about eighteen, and up at Oxford, when he lost his father. Izaak gives Thomas a high character, and the letters here presented confirm and in some ways extend it.

Before calling attention to some particular traits shown in these letters, which Thomas wrote during the last twelve years of his life, it is necessary to give the history of the volume in which they were found. It must be prolix, but it is desirable to authenticate a book which has lain unseen in one place for over three and a half centuries.

The letter-book contains 565 pages, 12½ by 8⅝ inches, and is bound in vellum, with Thomas's arms stamped in gold on both covers.[1] The first fifty pages bear a vertical rule in the middle, and were clearly intended for an index; it was never made, because Thomas died when only fifty pages had been closely filled. It will be found that a few letters are not in chronological sequence (e.g. Nos. IV and V); the possible explanation of this is that where the blank space on a page was inadequate for the next letter, it was copied on to the following page, and the vacant space was filled by a shorter letter of later date. In printing Roman numerals have been added for convenience of reference. Wotton also used the volume as a commonplace-book; thus there is a letter, of little interest on the face of it, which had been written to his father over twenty years before; there is 'Good Councell' to the Protector Somerset, who had been executed fully twenty-five years before, and there are some scathing lines on Parry, who was hanged in 1585.

The only one of Wotton's letters actually sent which has been

---

[1] The nine quarterings are attributed to their appropriate families in a note which follows the genealogical chart.

found so far is amongst the Lansdowne MSS. By the courtesy
of the British Museum it is shown at page 60, and the next plate
reproduces the copy in the letter-book. It will be seen that
Wotton caused a compliment to be added before signing it. That,
and the day of the month, were not added to the copy which had
already been made in the book. All the letters are in the same
beautiful script, except Nos. VIII to X, which are in another
hand. Wotton's own handwriting occurs nowhere.

Thomas died on 11 January 1587, five months after the date
of the last letter; at some time during the next twelve years it
passed into the possession of William Tothill,[1] one of the Six
Clerks in Chancery. It seems probable that the book may have
been taken to Tothill, who had chambers above his office which
occupied the site where Stone's Buildings now stand, in con-
nexion with some legal point. Thomas had twice been Sheriff
of Kent, the second time in 1578, and some of his letters reflect
his shrieval duties. Thomas's son Edward was Sheriff in 1594,
and may have taken the book to the Six Clerks' Office, as the
issue of warrants for Sheriffs was one of the duties of the Six
Clerks. Alternatively, the Six Clerks in those days acted as
ordinary solicitors,[2] and Edward (later knighted and finally
made a peer) may have consulted Tothill on the subject of the
very last letter, in which his father names him.

However the book passed into his possession, Mr. Tothill
found he had a very handsome volume little used, and on p. 91
he wrote in his own hand:

Marche 1° Anno 1599
Mine owne letters

He then copied into the book two most flowery letters to 'My
faire and Sweete Cousin', who is called 'Mrs J. H^ds' in the margin.
One letter says that since he saw her last 'you are a wyfe and
almost a mother'; her maiden name is therefore unknown and
she cannot be identified. The letters are not worth printing.

Tothill tired of this, and passed the book over to his clerks,

---

[1] Some account of him will be found in *Records of Bucks*, vol. xiv, and in *Shardeloes Papers*, 1947. Here it will suffice to say that he was son of Richard Tothill,
who printed *Tottel's Miscellany* in 1557; later he became rich by legal printing.

[2] Smith's *Chancery Practice*, p. 62. On 24 Oct. 1663 Mr. Pepys went to the Six
Clerks' Office 'and discoursed with my attorney and solicitor'.

The bay-window in the present dining-room, *c.* 1565

Interior doorway, early sixteenth century

and they wrote in standard forms of writs, warrants, &c., where precedent had to be followed. One form is for the appointment of a sheriff: 'Patent. Vicecomit.' Just before this time he had inherited from his father a considerable estate in Buckinghamshire, and in 1595 he added to it by purchasing the manor of Shardeloes, which adjoined it. Tothill retained his chambers in London, but between terms visited Shardeloes, and perhaps acted as solicitor for his neighbours, as leases were copied into the book of properties near to his but not in his own possession. This went on until a year or two after his death in 1626. The book was never used again and 300 pages remain clean and spotless as when new.[1]

Tothill's daughter married Francis Drake in 1602, and his descendants remained at Shardeloes, although they rebuilt the house on the old site in 1758–66. Some commonplace books in Tothill's writing were taken out of the house about 1900,[2] but this was unseen or disregarded, and was never amongst the mass of family muniments. When the house was eventually emptied of all contents in very recent years, many books and papers of little worth were found in cupboards, and taken to the residence of Mr. Francis Tyrwhitt-Drake, who is in the eleventh generation from Tothill. There the present editor found it, concealed in several dirty wrappings; Mr. Tyrwhitt-Drake continued the unfailing kindness which his late brother and himself have always shown, by entrusting it to his custody.

After full apology for this long and tedious history of the book, something must now be said about the letters and their writer.

On 17 August 1573 Queen Elizabeth, when making a Progress in Kent, visited Thomas Wotton at Boughton Malherbe. During that trip she met or visited several to whom letters will be found: Parker, Archbishop of Canterbury, William, Lord Cobham, Henry, Lord Bergavenny, and John Tufton, of Hothfield.[3] On this occasion Walton says that Thomas Wotton 'had many

---

[1] The watermark is an orb surmounted by a plain cross, with a label beneath bearing a number. Expert opinion thinks that the paper is of continental origin; it is not English.

[2] See *Records of Bucks*, vol. xiv, p. 167.

[3] Nichols's *Progresses etc.*, 1788, vol. i, p. 32.

invitations from Queen Elizabeth to change his . . . retirement for a Court, offering him a knighthood . . . and that to be but as an earnest of some more honourable and profitable employment, yet he humbly refused both'. Letter No. II was written in the very next year, and shows that he had been offered, and had declined, an appointment in Ireland. The emphatic expressions with which the letter closes prove his sincerity in declining the proposed honour.

Walton does not mention that Edward VI had actually named Wotton for the Knighthood of the Bath, but the young king died before Thomas was admitted to the Order, and his half-sister had other views. On 19 September 1553 the Privy Council sent 'a lettre to Thomas Wotton esquier, discharging hym from being Knight of the Bathe, whereunto he was once appointed and written unto'.[1] In 1549 Thomas's uncle, the Dean, was made Secretary of State to Edward VI, but resigned it after a few months to make room for Sir William Cecil, afterwards the great Lord Burleigh. Is it possible that the Dean was himself ineligible for the honour, but requested it for his favourite nephew? Letters XVII, LII, and LVI show that Thomas was on very good terms with Lord Burleigh.

Wotton was also very friendly with the Earl of Leicester and with Sir Francis Walsingham, both of whom showed favour to the early nonconformists, who aroused Wotton's sympathies most deeply. According to the *Shorter Oxford Dictionary*, the word nonconformist first occurs about thirty years after Wotton's death, but its original meaning about covers the way in which it is applied here:

One who, while adhering to the Church of England, refused to conform to its discipline and practice.

Thomas Wotton owned several advowsons, and duly made presentations to them. The evidence afforded by the letters with regard to his own views is that Nos. I and XXXVIII show that he was friendly towards two of the most prominent non-conformists. No. XIX exhibits his confidence in preachers on market-days doing much 'towarde thamendement of men's

[1] *Acts of the Privy Council, 1552–4*, p. 351.

maners', No. XXXIV pleads for the widow of a preacher, and
No. LIV supports the petition of the Kentish clergy who had
not publicly accepted the Thirty-nine Articles.

Of the fifty-seven letters written by Thomas Wotton very
nearly a third relate to the troubles of other people who had no
obvious claim on him. No. XVII seeks Lord Burleigh's help for
two heirs to an estate with a weak title. No. XVIII exhorts
a debtor to deal justly with his creditors, whilst No. XXVIII
appeals to a creditor to be merciful to his debtor. No. XLVI
pleads for a man who is not named. No. LV protests against an
attempt to prejudice a father against his son. Nos. XVI and XX
were written by way of eirenicon where his friends were at
variance.

These are typical of the way in which Thomas Wotton's
kindly nature led him to use his great influence in the county for
the benefit of all who were in distress. Whilst asking nothing for
himself, he did not shrink from asking for others; he might
almost be called a Complete Altruist, from the letter-book.
Walton says: 'This Thomas . . . was a cherisher of learning, as
appears by that excellent antiquary Mr William Lambarde, in his
Perambulation of Kent.' The third edition of that work, published in 1570, bears a long dedication to Thomas in which
Lambard says: 'you came first to my minde, for the good understanding and interest you have in this shire.' The edition of 1576
includes a letter addressed by Wotton himself to 'His Countrie-
men, the Gentlemen of the Countye of Kent', and an extract from
it is given:

I know not how I may more fitly and effectually commend it thē to
say, that it is in substance an hystorie, treating of the partes (and
actions of greatest weight a good time together, done by the most
famous persons), of one, speciall Countrie; set frõ great antiquitie,
which many men are much delighted with; out of sundry bookes with
great studie collected painfully; by this authoure in the matter set out,
truely; with good words wel placed, eloquently. . . .

I muste needes say that (the sacred word of Almightie God always
excepted), there is nothing either for our instruction more profitable,
or to our mindes more delectable, or within the compasse of common
understanding more easie or facile, then the studie of hystories.

Wotton closes with an allusion to another work which Lambarde began, but did not complete,[1] and says:

surely, being as he is unto mee a very deere freende, for myne awne parte I meane also (God willing) upon some fit occasion to further it. The xvj of Aprill 1576 Your Countreyman and very loving friende, T.W.

A controversial book dedicated to Thomas Wotton was a reply to Bishop Jewell written by Edward Dering in 1568; it bears a long title beginning *A Sparing Restrainte . . .'*.[2]

Apart from these proofs that Wotton was 'a cherisher of learning', there is ample evidence that he acquired a good library, which remained at Broughton Malherbe until the fourth Earl of Chesterfield, who had inherited it, removed the books to Bretby. There they remained until 1919, when they were sold at Sotheby's on 8 July. Some were acquired by Mr. J. W. Hely-Hutchinson, who published an account of them by Mr. H. M. Nixon in a Roxburghe Club volume, 1953.[3]

The magnificent plates in colour show the fine French bindings, apparently made soon after Thomas inherited his estates in 1551. Mr. Nixon shows that none is of later date than the end of 1552. The ten-volume edition of Erasmus, printed at Basle in 1540, is particularly beautiful; each volume has in the centre of the covers: 'Thomae Wottoni et amicorum'.[4] Other volumes bear this ownership inscription, and some bear his arms, with four quarterings. The learned detail with which Mr. Nixon traces the ownership of these noble calf bindings must be read in full in the Roxburghe volume; here it need only be said that he makes it clear that after Wotton settled in Kent, he had his books bound in England, in plain calf or vellum, with the armorial

[1] Lambarde discontinued his topographical account of England and Wales, when he heard that Camden was engaged on his great work. In 1730 Lambarde's MS., edited by his descendant Multon Lambarde, was printed by Fletcher Gyles.

[2] The *D.N.B.* says that *The Christian State of Matrimony*, by Thomas Becon, was dedicated to Wotton. The edition of 1543 has a note to the effect that it was Coverdale's translation of a work by J. Bullinger and that Becon wrote the preface. Wotton's name does not appear, indeed he was far too young, but it was reprinted in 1575, and later. These editions have not been seen.

[3] A copy of the folio edition of Chaucer, 1542, was sold at Christie's in July 1959. The fine binding bears the words 'Thomae Wottoni et amicorum' in a central panel, but there are no arms. The signature of Robert Rudston appears more than once. He was related to Wotton's first wife, whose mother was widow of Sir John Rudston, Lord Mayor in 1528, when she married Sir Edward Wotton, as his second wife.

[4] These fine volumes are now in Eton College Library.

stamp bearing nine quarterings, the same as appears on our letter-book.

One book from Thomas's library is now in possession of the Walters Art Gallery, Baltimore; it is a folio copy of Nicole Gilles's *Les . . . annales et croniques . . . des beligueses Gaulles*, Paris, 1551.[1]

Besides the original letter to Lord Burleigh already mentioned, the British Museum has another from Wotton to him, when Sir William Cecil.[2] It is dated 13 June 1563 and concerns the widow and children of Sir Thomas Finch, who was half-brother of Wotton's second wife and had just been lost at sea. The British Museum also holds two letters from Wotton to Richard Dering. The first is dated 27 December 1583,[3] and is an attempt by Wotton to stop a lawsuit between Mr. Harlackenden and Mr. Bettenham over a right of way. Richard, whom Wotton calls 'My good Dick,' had succeeded his father John at Surrenden Dering in 1550, and lived until 1612, dying aged eighty-two.[4] The second letter is dated 21 August 1586,[5] and is a very humble apology for having given his 'good cousin' a very bad dinner at Boughton—it had been a matter of much grief to Wotton ever since.

There is no letter from Wotton in the Bodleian Library, nor is there any in the County Record Office at Maidstone. Some archives of the City of Canterbury are deposited in the Chapter Library of that city, and among them are two holograph letters and a receipt by Wotton dated 1555.[6] Thomas was granting the fee farm of some property to the City for £20 a year, and wrote: 'Y am wel contentyd to stande unto the bargayne I have made with my masters of Cantorburye for my fee farme.'

In printing the letters the modern use of i and j and of u and v has been followed, and ff, used as a capital, is represented by F.

The writing of the book is so excellent that, apart from the slips which attend all human efforts, the editor hopes that he is

---

[1] From information most kindly given to the editor by Miss Dorothy Miner, Librarian, in a letter of 22 Sept. 1958.
[2] Lansdowne MSS. 7.   [3] Stowe MSS. 150, f. 31.
[4] Hasted, vol. iii, p. 229. John Dering, of Egerton, fourth son of John of Surrenden, married Elizabeth, daughter of Thomas Wotton, as his second wife. Hasted, iii. 221.   [5] Stowe MSS. 150, f. 51.
[6] The editor is indebted to Dr. W. Urry, F.S.A., for kindly bringing these early letters to his notice.

presenting a faithful text of the letters. He is far more diffident about the notes which he has appended to the letters, owing to the complete ignorance of Kent with which he began to annotate the letters eighteen months ago.

Wotton was not a graceful letter-writer. The reader stumbles amongst a litter of sub-clauses, or is faced with one of the triple predications so dear to Wotton. For all that, the syntax will not be found at fault. The stately formality of Wotton's style contrasts strongly with the directness of his correspondents Burleigh, Walsingham, and Leicester; they wasted no words in making their points.

Wotton's spelling is more consistent, on the whole, than that of his contemporaries. No spelling is peculiar to himself, but he invariably wrote 'myne awne' for 'my own', whilst Leicester usually wrote 'my none', and sometimes 'myne owen'. Wotton wrote 'othe' where we write 'oath', but the Earl of Warwick wrote it 'awthe'.

Whoever has the patience to read the letters through will become acquainted with a man of strong character, austere, and utterly devoid of humour. These are not sociable qualities, but they are balanced by the readiness with which he applied his great influence at Court, or in his native county, to the relief of those who were in trouble and lacked a friend. To the editor this seems evidence of a good heart; a cynic might call it pride's delight to exercise power. At all events he was quite free from worldly ambitions, and one wonders whether his youngest son, Sir Henry, had not his father in mind when he wrote:[1]

> Unti'd unto the World by care
> Of publick Fame or privat Breath;
> Who envies none that chance doth raise.

Great Canfield   G. E.
March 1960

THANKS

THE Marc Fitch Fund kindly assumed responsibility for much of the cost of printing this book, and so made its appearance possible at this time. The editor is sincerely grateful for the Fund's generous support.

[1] From *A Character of a Happy Life*, said to have been written in 1614. There are various readings; the wording above is that of *Reliquiae Wottonianae*, 1685 edition.

SCHEDULE OF THE LETTERS

ILLUSTRATIONS

The editor thanks Charles Bounds for the fine photographs of Boughton Place. He made the journey from Glamorgan to Kent on purpose to take them, and in proof of an unbroken friendship of twenty-seven years.

CHART SHOWING MEMBERS OF WOTTON FAMILY MENTIONED

(The numbers in brackets refer to the arms on the next page)

Sir Nicholas Wotton, Lord Mayor 1416 and 1431, died 14 Sept. 1448 == Joan Corby (1), heiress of Boughton Malherbe, Sheriffs Court Minster, &c.

Nicholas Wotton, died 9 Apr. 1499 Brass in church == Elizabeth Bamburgh (2), heiress of Padlesworth near Snodland

Sir Robert Wotton, born 1465, Sheriff 1498, Comptroller of Calais == Anne Belknap (3–4–5–6), heiress of St Mary Cray and of Ringwould

Sir Edw. Wotton P.C., born 1489, Sheriff 1529 and 1535, Treasurer of Calais. Died 1551 == 1st Dorothy Reade (7–8–9), heiress of Chiddingstone Died 8 Sept. 1529 / 2nd Ursula Dymock, widow of Sir John Rudstone

Nicholas Wotton P.C., Dean of York and of Canterbury, Ambassador many times. Died 25 Jan. 1567

Margaret Wotton == 1st William Medley 2nd Thomas Grey, Earl of Dorset

Thomas Wotton, born 1521, Sheriff 1558 and 1578, died 11 Jan. 1587 o.s. == 1st Elizabeth, dau. of Sir John Rudstone / 2nd Eleanor, dau. of Sir William Finch and widow of Henry Morton

William Wotton == Mary Dannet

Edward Wotton, Comptr of Household and knight 1601. Treasurer of Household and Lord Wotton 1616. Died 1618. == 1st Hester, natural dau. of Sir Wm Pickering 2nd Margaret dau. of Philip Lord Wharton

John Wotton, b. 1550, Knt. 1591 == Luce, dau. of Henry, Earl of Northumberland. Died 1597

James Wotton, Knight 1596. Died 1628

Sir Henry Wotton, born 30 Mar. 1568, Ambassador to Venice, &c. Provost of Eton. Died Dec. 1639.

xviii

THE ARMS ON THE LETTER-BOOK

SIR NICHOLAS the Lord Mayor bore as arms: Argent a cross patée fitchée sable. His wife Joan Corby was a considerable heiress, and her son, Nicholas II, dropped the cross patée and used the Corby arms: Argent a saltire engrailed sable.[1] This practice was continued during the next four generations. Thomas placed nine quarterings on the monument which he raised to his uncle the Dean in Canterbury Cathedral, and they were stamped on the books which he had bound in England, including the letter-book. They also appear on his mural monument in the chancel of the Church above his bust, which Gray would not have called 'animated'. They are as follows:

No. of quarterings	Heiress	Arms
1	Corby	Ar. a saltire engrailed sa.
2	Bamburgh	Ar. on a chief sa., a lion passant
3	Belknap	On a bend 3 eaglets displayed bet. 2 cotises ar.
4	Butler	Gu. a fesse checky, a. & s., bet. 6 crosses, formée, fitchée.
5	Sudeley	Ar. 2 bends gu.
6	Mountfort	Bendy of 10 pieces, ar. & az.
7	Reade	Gu. on a bend wavy ar., 3 shovellers sa.
8	Alphew	Ar. a fosse bet. 3 boars' heads sa.
9	Petit	A chevron engrailed gu., bet. 3 horns sa.

Dr. W. Urry, F.S.A., most kindly furnished a photostat of a pedigree which is in the Chapter Library, Canterbury. It was made about 1623 and extends to the second, and last, Lord Wotton and his daughters, then infants. Sixteen quarters are carefully tricked, and their identification is easy.

[1] The original grant of these arms is given in Camden's *Remains Concerning Britain*. It is dated 6 Jan. 1349 and is addressed to 'mon bon amee Robert de Corby et à ces heires'.

'MY HOWSE IN BOCTON MALHERBE'

The male line of Wotton ended with Thomas's grandson, the second Lord Wotton. His eldest daughter married Henry, Lord Stanhope, and she was eventually made Countess of Chesterfield for her life. Subsequent descents need not be given here, but the last Stanhope owner was the famous letter-writer and wit, the fourth Earl of Chesterfield. In 1750 he sold Boughton Malherbe to Galfridus Mann, of Linton. Horace Walpole reported it to his 'dear Gal's' brother Sir Horace on 2 August, and two years later he tried to see 'the remains of a house of the Wottons', but he arrived when it was growing dark.[1] By 1782 Hasted reported 'but small remains of the mansion left standing, the greatest part of it having been pulled down many years ago, and what is left only sufficient for a farmhouse'.[2]

Only the west wing remained but until 1922 it contained exceptionally fine panelling, consisting of 350 large panels, finely carved with Gothic ornament, and early Renaissance medallions. It had been placed there by Thomas's father, Sir Edward, before 1529, because one panel bore his initials and those of his wife who died in that year. They were seen and admirably illustrated by Mr. H. Avray Tipping.[3]

In very recent years the shell of this once lovely house fell into the hands of those who are preserving what remains, and some illustrations show work which may cover the Wotton ownership down to the time of our letter-writer. The small doorway in the west front, if rightly dated, may be the work of Sir Nicholas, the Lord Mayor. The windows above it are of much later date, and may be ascribed to Sir Edward, who may also be responsible for the interior doorway. The large oriel and all north of it were the work of Thomas, carried out before Queen Elizabeth's visit, except the northernmost addition in brick; the date 1584 is now inside the end wall.

The fourth plate at page 60 shows a niche which, though much defaced, is of great interest, as it appears to be similar to one at

---

[1] Letter to Bentley, 5 Aug. 1752.   [2] Hasted, vol. ii, p. 432.
[3] *English Homes II*, vol. i. pp. 213–29. Mr. C. Hussey, F.S.A. is sincerely thanked for calling attention to this valuable article.

CISTERN AND LAVATORY

(b) Lavatorium at Battel Hall, Leeds, fourteenth century

(a) Defaced niche at Boughton Place, early fifteenth century

Battel Hall, Leeds, which is within six miles of Boughton Place. A fine drawing of the more perfect specimen at Leeds is reproduced, to save written description.[1] It was the medieval form of a washhand basin; the rectangular trough shown at Leeds has disappeared at Boughton, as well as the elaborate carving of foliage outside the ogee and the leafy crest. Perhaps they were roughly hacked off when the wall was panelled. As the cusps are more crudely cut than the fine work at Leeds, the Boughton Place example may be of the first half of the fifteenth century in the time of Sir Nicholas.

[1] It is from Turner and Parker's *Domestic Architecture, etc.*, 1853, vol. ii, pp. 46 and 285. Battel Hall is a part, possibly of the Guest House, of Leeds Priory.

I. *To the right worshipfull his very assured loving frende,*
Mr Docto^r Humfreys

Sir, for your great curtesye many wayes shewed to meself and for my sake unto sondrye of my frendes, I doo most hartelye thanke you. And right sorye wolde I be that the preferment of any one sholde procure you the displeasure of any other, and namely of her most excellent Matie. My requestes that without intermission come daylye maye not otherwyse be done, then you maye doo theym convenyently.

If Sir Anthony Cooke were eyther the man that afore the Lorde he ought to be, or afore the worlde wolde seeme to be, in so great age, in so blessed dayes, in Sutes farre from lawe, farther from equitie, he wolde never doo as he dothe. This he sayethe shortly, that (albeit he be a partie), sayethe therin truly. By his speciall meanes I have of late ben very hardely handeled, the particuler declaration wherof wolde make a longer letter then I meane this shall be.

A good gentleman of this Countrye wyll shortly have here in hande a free Schoole, unto the master of the Schoole when the woorke ys finisshed wyll he geve yerely xx^{li} and the nomination of the schoolemaster dothe he leave unto me. An honest man for conscience sake I maye not, an unlerned man for shame I dare not be a Judge of the Schoolemaster's sufficiencye, and therfore when the nomination of hym shall come unto me, I recken to admyt suche a one as for that purpose shall come commended from you. I doe for my parte in this man first of all desyre that in profession he maye be a knowen, zelous christian man, and secondely in naturall disposition (farre from rage or furye), a mylde and pacient man. I doo also for my parte thincke yt meete that the nomber of his Schollers (by the founder's appoyntment brought to a certayntie), sholde be suche as the master might rather sufficiently instructe a fewe, then slightly instructe a manye. In this poynt specially, and in suche other thinges as you thincke meete for this Schoole generallye, I praye you at your convenyent leysure let me have your opinion. And this with my right hartie commendations for this tyme, I take my leave of you from my howse in Bocton Malherbe, the vth of August, 1574, your assured loving frende.

Lawrence Humphrey was Regius Professor of Divinity at Oxford; when this letter was written he was Dean of Gloucester, later Dean of Winchester. He went to Zurich during the reign of Queen Mary, and on his return he counted as a leader of the early 'nonconformists'. He was a close friend of John Fox and of Thomas Cartwright (see No. XXXVIII). As he was 'a great scholar, able linguist, and deep divine', he managed to keep his church preferment.[1] His dislike of vestments extended to academic robes, but he put on his scarlet gown when Queen Elizabeth visited Oxford in 1566. She noticed it, told him that it became him ('haec vestis te quam optime decet'), and wondered why he did not wear it more often, but she did not wish to chide him ('sed criminari nunc temporis nolo').[2] He died in 1590.

Sir Anthony Cooke had been one of the tutors of Edward VI, and was first professor of Greek at Cambridge. His four daughters were all 'learned ladies',[3] and made good marriages: Mildred was wife of Lord Burleigh, Anna was wife of Sir Nicholas Bacon and therefore mother of Lord Verulam, Elizabeth first married Sir Thomas Hoby, and, after his death, John, son of the Earl of Bedford. Katherine married Sir Henry Killigrew. A large and imposing monument in Romford Church has the kneeling effigies of the whole family.

There is no doubt that the school for which Wotton sought a master was that at Sandwich, founded between 1563 and 1584 on a site near the Canterbury Gate, largely by the energy of Sir Roger Manwood, who retained for himself during his lifetime the rents of the lands with which he had 'endowed' the school, but paid the master's stipend of £20 a year.[4] Some account of Manwood is given in a note to No. XLIII.

II. *To his very loving frende Mr. Owen Moore*

My deere frende, for your curteous Letters of the vth of June (by the handes of Mr Gowge brought unto me in the last of Julye) I doo right hartely thanke you.

That wynde that out of Englande blowe into Irelande a

---

[1] Wood, *Athen. Oxon.*, vol. i, cols. 558–61.
[2] Wood, *Hist. Univ. Oxon.*, 1674, p. 287.
[3] Ballard, *Memoirs of British Ladies*, 1775, pp. 126–47.
[4] Boys, *Collections for a History of Sandwich*, 1792.

reaporte of my commyng thither caryed a matter begonne with greater hast then speede. I am not (I thanke god) so ambitious as that for a little honoure. I sholde takeupon me an office of greater weight then my shoulders ar hable to beare, and so eyther fall and shame mee self, (whiche were yll), or by simple service for lacke of good knowledge hynder her Matie and the Realme (whiche were woorse).

And therfore farre from the courte and matters of state, brought up (as you knowe) in the Countrye about Countrye causes (and of all others best knowne to meeself), I have for myne excuse and discharge alleaged that thing trulye, that (constraned by the duitie of a good Subjecte) I was (me thought) bounde to saye playnlye and effectuallye. And so here am I, and while god shall suffer me to lyve (I hope) here shall you fynde me, in a meane estate contented wythe that that the Lorde hathe sent me, being many wayes moche more then I have deserved, and every waye as moche as I desyre. And thus wythe my right hartie commendačons, I wyshe you alwayes right hartely well to fare. From my howse in Bocton Malherbe the xith of August 1574. your assured frende.

Owen Moore was the eldest son of John Moore, of Moore Court, Benenden. His next brother was Edward, knighted in camp by Sir William Drury, 1579.

They are named in a letter from Sir Henry Sidney to Arthur, Lord Grey, when Lord Deputy of Ireland, dated 17th September 1580: 'I had forgotten three kinsmen of my own, Sir Edward More, Owen More (eldest), and Thomas More.'[1]

Had Wotton been offered the position of Lord Deputy, in the absence of Sir Henry Sidney, who was reappointed to that office in 1575?

III. *To the most worshipfull his very assured loving cousyn John Astley Esquire, Master of her Ma^{tie's} Jewell howse*

Against your owne appoyntment to be thus long absent ys a matter greevous unto us. Bycause we feare that thoccasion therof

---

[1] Historical MSS. Comm. Report, Ser. 77, vol. ii, p. 94 (1934); *Archaeologia Cantiana*, vol. lviii, p. 18.

ys greevous unto you. And therfore Desirous to heare from you, we have sent this bearer unto you, by whom we wolde be right gladde to knowe that you meane (yf the lorde so wyll), shortly to be here.

Untill you come your self, your busynesse (requyring your owne advise and good direction), must eyther stande still in the state they ar in (whiche were yll), or happely proceede unorderly (whiche were woorse). And therfore the sooner you come, in estate the better wyll yt be unto you. In mynde the more joyfull wyll yt be unto us. Untill which tyme I doe thus take my leave of you, From my howse in Bocton Malherbe the xjth of Januarye 1574, your assured loving cousyn.

John Astley, Master of the Queen's Jewel House, was granted the manor of Newnham Court, Boxley, in 1569 for a term of years (it had been forfeited to the Crown by Wyatt's attainder); he died in 1595.[1] He was present at the Windsor dinner of 1563, so well described by Ascham in the preface to the *Scholemaster*, but 'M. Astley said verie litle'.

His son of the same name was knighted and granted lands in Otterden and Allington Castle.

IV. *To the right worshipfull his very loving frende Thomas Potter Esquire*

The slacke execution of thorder lately taken at Maydestone (emong all the Justicers of the peace resiaunt within the Lathe of Sutton at Hone) hathe made the burdeyne so weightie unto us as we can no longer beare yt.

If this thing (being in use for theym that sholde have yt very needefull, in consent emong those that were there then present, after good advise universall in christian purpose by those that sholde geve yt, very charitable; in collection by those that sholde gather yt very easye or facile),—yf this thing (I saye) thus good, upon theese causes thus grounded, be thus slightly overpassed I knowe not what thing I shall hope to see duely perfourmed. And therfore surely for myne owne parte (making this matter always a good president for myne excuse), I meane no more for

---

[1] *D.N.B.* and Hasted, vol. ii, p. 127.

the common cause of our Countrey to be at any common assemblea. Where the thing concerneth all in generall, the charge wolde not be borne (as hitherto yt hathe ben), by a fewe in particuler.

Hereof I thought meete to advertise you, as one that I knowe hathe a good mynde to helpe yt. And for your being moche at home, ys afore other of your fellowes lyke to deale in yt. From my howse in Bocton Malherbe the xv^th of Marche 1574, your assured frende.

Thomas Potter belonged to a family dwelling at Well Street, Westerham, since 1364. He died on 13 February 1612, leaving a widow, Elizabeth. His daughter and heir married Sir John Rivers[1] (see No. XXVIII).

Sutton at Hone is the westernmost of the five lathes, or administrative areas, into which Kent was divided. Thomas Wotton had a house at St. Mary Cray (see note to No. XII), which made him resident in that lathe, though his chief house at Boughton Malherbe was in the lathe of Aylesford.

V. *To the right honorable his very assured loving frende Sir Henry Sydney, Knight of the most honorable Order of the Garter, Lorde President of Wales*

Sir, being so neere you as I am, I maye be moche asshamed (where I might come mee self), thus to wryte unto you as I doo. But surelie my busynesse of thone syde, and the bytternesse of this weather of thother syde, doo constrayne me to holde me selfe at home. The wyfe of your servaunt Mr Thomas Fynche hathe, wythe good woordes in a very lamentable sorte, sondrye tymes desyred mee to be a meane unto hym that he wolde unto hym selfe agayne receyve her, and as his good wyfe, (whiche wythe solempne protestation shee hathe promised to be), agayne to entreate her. And yf he might not be brought unto that (whiche of all other thinges shee dyd principallye desyre), that he wolde then yet towarde her releefe with some thing lovynglye consider her. At her request upon this respecte I have twyse or thryse therin rather spoken unto hym, then effectuallye perswaded hym.

[1] Hasted, vol. i, p. 386. *Archaeologia Cantiana*, vol. xx, p. 7.

And now shee thinckethe (and so doo I too), that yf yt might please your good Lordeshippe therin to deale wythe hym, he wyll at your motion (or els at the motion of none), doo that that therin surelye he ys bounde to doo. Howe shee hathe towarde hym heretofore used her selfe I knowe not. But surelye in speache and demeanure shee seemethe nowe well stayed and vertuouslye disposed. And poore shee ys, and here in a very harde sorte passethe many a heavye daye, wherof (thus warned), hee sholde mee thinckethe in conscience have some remorse. Towarde whiche I doo most humblie beseeche your good Lordeshippe as effectuallye as ye maye to move hym. Shee shall therfore be deeply bounde to praye for you, the Lorde wyll of his mercye therfore rewarde you. And thus I beseeche God to sende you good and long lyfe, and moche encrease of honoure. From my howse in London the xix^th of Februarye 1573. Your most bounden.

Sir Henry Sidney was made Lord President of the Marches of Wales in 1560. He had been Lord Justice of Ireland in 1557, and Lord Deputy in 1558 and 1565, and once more in 1575, whilst continuing to be Lord President of Wales.

Thomas Finch was connected with Sir Thomas Finch, who was half-brother of Wotton's second wife. When Sir Thomas was made knight marshal in the fighting about Havre in 1563, he sent 'his kinsman Thomas to act as provost marshal'.[1]

Wotton's appeal for Mrs. Thomas Finch may well have reminded Sidney of a case in which he had been consulted twenty years before. The story has been preserved by no less a writer than Bacon,[2] and would be spoiled by abbreviation. 'Secretary Bourn's son kept a gentleman's wife in Shropshire, who lived from her husband, with him; when he was weary of her, he caused her husband to be dealt with to take her home, and offered him five hundred pounds for reparation; the gentleman went to Sir H. Sidney to take his advice upon this offer telling him, "that his wife promised now a new life; and, to tell him truth, five hundred pounds would come well with him; and besides that sometimes he wanted a woman in his bed". "By my troth," said Sir Henry Sidney, "take her home, and take the money; and then whereas other cuckolds wear their horns plain, you may wear yours gilt." '

---

[1] Bryan I'Anson, *History of the Finch Family*, 1933, pp. 20 and 46.
[2] *Apophthegm*, 44. Sir John Bourne was Secretary of State to Queen Mary, 1553.

VI. *To the right honorable his very good Lorde the Arche-bisshoppe of Canterburye his grace*

My good Lorde,

I am right sorye to heare by howe many good and wyse men howe moche yt ys upon good respectes generallye myslyked that poore Bonham (in profession a christian man, in conversation a vertuous man), for such a thing (yf I shall under your correction playnlye saye my opinion), as by good wytnesses against hym apparently proved (whiche I here yet this thing ys not), sholde in qualitie and quantitie of offence amount to a meane matter, be so hardelye handeled, that after a course of so long imprisonment, he maye neyther be favorablye delyvered, nor upon good Bonde any wayes bayled. The knowledge I have of your good wysdome and good nature dothe encourage mee, and the pitie I have of the poore man and the duitye I owe unto almightie god, doo constrayne mee to commende hym and the releefe of his heavye lyfe unto you. Towarde whom I doo most humblie beseeche you, Sir, wythe some good speede to extende so moche of your good favoure as his Innocencye in the thing, and his honestye gener-allye in all thinges doo justlye deserve. And thus I beseeche the Lorde to sende you good and long lyfe, and the contynuaunce of moche honoure. From my howse in London the xiij^th of June 1574, your most bounden

The Archbishop was Matthew Parker, but the 'long lyfe' which Wotton hoped he might have was very near its close; he died within a year, on 17 May 1575.

The minister Bonham, for whom Wotton pleads, may be he who is named with seven others by Fuller[1] at this date, as amongst the earliest 'nonconformists'. Their objections were against vestments and the book of Common Prayer, rather than 'a new discipline' on presbyterian lines.

---

[1] *Church History*, book ix, sect. 3, § 9.

VII. *To the right honorable his very assured loving frende Frauncis Walsingham Esquire, one of her Maties principall Secretaryes*

Sir, the bearer hereof my cousyn Thomas Cobham hathe upon good cause by action commenced and (with an orderly course of pleading), continued afore the Mayre and Jurates of Dovour so farre furthe recovered against the wydowe of Peper as therin he lackethe onlye his execution, whiche, upon a vayne surmise or twayne in favoure of the wydowe (I beleeve surelye against the lawe), was at the last court daye holden there put of untill Mondaye the   of the next   And nowe he hearethe that towarde the right honourable the Lordes of her Maties most honorable preevye Councell shee hathe alredye made, or shortly meanethe to make a speciall sute for a longer staye of the said execution, whiche thing, in the state he standethe, (having I knowe lyttle to lyve upon), and in the state the wydowe her self standethe,—being a person of very great yeres, wolde be unto hym a matter of very great hynderaunce. And therfore, as one of his frendes I doo most humblie beseeche you, Sir, to be herein good unto hym. So well dothe he thincke of the partes of his cause (and for my parte surely so doo I too), that he can be right well contented that your self alone, or the right honorable the Lordes of her Maties most honorable Councell, shall appoynt one or ij, or moe, to heare yt and (yf they can) finallye to ende yt, so alwayes yt mate be done afore the said   of the next   . And this thing (consydered by the state he standethe in, and by the state the cause yt selfe standethe in), shewethe hymselfe to be a personne desyrous in a quyet sorte to possesse his awne. Towarde whiche I doo most humblie beseeche you, Sir, let hym have your reasonable and lawfull favoure. And thus I beseeche the Lorde to sende you good and long lyfe, and thincrease of moche honoure. From my howse in London the xxi^th of Aprill **1575**, your assured lovyng frende

Thomas seems to be the 'scapegrace brother' of William, tenth Lord Cobham (to whom Nos. XXVI, XXXV, and XLV are addressed). As Lord Warden of the Cinque Ports, Lord Cobham had to examine a supporter of Mary Queen of Scots, at the time of the Duke of Norfolk's trial, 1572, and found papers which he proposed to lay before the Council. Thomas was involved in this, and actually arrested and sent to the Tower. Ultimately he was pardoned.[1] He married Katherine, daughter of Sir William Cavendish.[2]

VIII. *To the right worshipfull Sir Edward Wotton, knight, highe Thesaurer of the Kings Maties Towne of Callyie and Mercher of the same*

Yf the torment of myn awne consience for myn offence com-mytted towardes yowr mastership were as good recompence unto yowe as it hathe ben punishemennt unto me, I might with some what more boldnes presennt this my humble peticion to th obteynynge of yowr perdon, but my faulte withowt purgation, and yowe therof hitherto unsatisfied, I have no other hope nor confidence but in yowr gentle, noble, and moderate nature, trustinge that like the pitieful father yowe will receyve me yor prodigall childe to mercye.
And thoughe that name be unpropriate unto mee, yet saval by yowr goodnesse havinge throughe myn awne fraylenes deserved ruyne, I cannot but call my selfe yo^rs in renovation, or released of yowr woorthie displeasure, I must neede counte yowe the authoure of my beynge, and owe yowe all that which maye in any wise come of mee. This twoo yeres consumed in Italie. I havinge spennt my tyme as I judge not altogether unproffitablie, and done one or two grateful services, I shall shortelie departe home wardes upon a good occasion commended with the letters of the Kinge's Highnesse Embassadour here.
I therfore nowe most humblie require your maistershipp to be unmyndefull of that I have deserved, and to release or at the leest suspend yowr displeasure till by some meanes I may justifie some parte of my facte, and I shall evermore unto yowr maister-ship be the same your servant and suche one as yor favorable

---

[1] *Archaeologia Cantiana*, xii. 134–49, article by J. G. Waller.
[2] Ibid. lxii. 55, article by R. H. D'Elboux.

goodnesse therin shall bynde me to be alwaies prayenge unto god for yor good preservation.

As nowe from Venice the xith of July,
Your maistershippes bedeman bounden evermore

John Brende

This letter differs from all the others by having been addressed to Sir Edward, Thomas Wotton's father. In July 1540 Henry VIII revived the office of Treasurer of Calais, and Sir Edward took up the appointment on 24 November in that year. He died on 8 November 1551.[1]

John Brend (alias William Watson), was Envoy to the Hanse Towns. On 24 January 1549 the Senate of Bremen wrote to Edward VI, with a copy to 'John Brend, H.M. Ambassador', agreeing not to supply the Scots with munitions or provisions. They casually add that they would be glad of a loan of 6,000 talents for a few years.[2]

IX. *To the right honorable owre verye good Lordes the Lordes of her Maties honorable privie councell*

Owre bounden duities unto yowr good Lordeshipps most humblie remembered. It maie please yowe to understande that by force of yowr Letters of the xxijth of Januarie this daie meetinge here we have examyned the substance and partes of that information that by Thomas Wandenne of this Towne, tailoure, was unto yowr good Lordeshippes exhibited against Rychard Ryve of the same Towne yeman. And fyndinge that the said information tooke his begynnynge rather from some greefe and displeasure conceyved and a longe tyme continued betweene theese ij parties, then from any yll thinge lately done by the said Rychard Ryve,—we moved theym to be and by owre motions (all former unkyndnesse on eche parte promised to be forgotten), they said they were contented to be eche towarde other good neighboures, and frendes. Whiche course in this thinge for owre partes (dwellinge neere the Towne, and for their partes dwellinge in the Towne), we thought more meete to take then towarde yowr good Lordeshippes by owre opynions as yt were to accuse

---

[1] From *D.N.B.* and other sources.
[2] *State Papers. Foreign. Edw. VI*, printed 1861.

the one and to excuse thother. And thus we beseeche the Lorde to sende unto yowr good Lordeshippes good and longe life and the continuaunce of moche honoure. From Maidstone the xiiij[th] of Marche 1576. Humblie at the Commandement of yowr good Lordeshippes.

		Thomas Wotton	Nicholas
Signed thus	Sentleger	Thomas
	Hendley	

This report had been called for by the Privy Council on 12 January.[1]

The signature Sentleger probably relates to Sir Warham St. Leger, of Ulcombe, of whom some account is given in a note to No. XXIX.

It is clear from No. XXXVI that Wandenne was a rogue.

X. *To the right honorable his verie good Lorde therle of Leycester*

My good Lorde,

If the Medleye mentioned in yo[r] letter be not Henrye or Wylliam (unto whom as bretherne descended of the same parenntes I am in nature a neere kynsman, and wher their causes be honest in Devotion a trewe frende),—then I neither knowe the man, nor ever herde of the man. The cause of his commyttinge, and therupon the commyttinge and brutes or reaportes after the commyttinge I am also altogether ignoraunt yn, and so I neither knowe the man nor the matter; neyther was I (nor this that I have said standinge trewe, coulde I be), the authoure of the letter that yowe wryt of. Yf under my name any one have unto your good Lordeshippe sennt suche a thinge as yowe receyve in good parte, in that yowe like it, I am (onelie yn respecte of that likinge), right gladde of it.

And yet that this matter (suche as it is) might have ben (as everie good matter ought to be) handeled after a good maner, I wolde have wyshed the partie him selfe under his owne name to have taken the praise and thanncks of his owne doynge. Touchinge suche brutes as tende to the infamie and suche accusations as tende to the perill of anye personne, syns I came to the consideracon of suche things as (emonge other) apperteyne to the

---

[1] *Acts of the Privy Council 1575-7*, p. 274.

Actions of an honest man, I have neither loved nor lightlie beleeved thone, nor used thother.

And therfore that bodie (what so ever he were), was smallie my frende, that under my name towarde a personne of so great estate and honoure as yowe ar woorthely of, wolde enter into a discourse of such things as upon good respectes I have a longe tyme moche misliked. This is in Medleye and in the woordes and deedes spoken and done by Medleye. And in the l̃re under my name written unto yowe concernynge reaportes made of Medleye, that that I knowe, that is all layed together (Henrie and William Medleye my cousins excepted),—nothinge at all. Wherof I wolde soner have written unto yowr good Lordeshippe. If yowr l̃re (by a ryppier yesterdaie brought unto mee), had soner come unto my handes.

Touchinge yowr goodnesse towarde mee, and my duitie towarde yowe, so many waies have yowe so honorablie used mee and Edward Wotton my sonne, and in the hearinge of the great cause that my good frende Mr Temple and I to owr great greefe had too longe a tyme in hande, so indifferentlie have ye caryed your selfe, as I must therfore while I lyve accompt mee selfe deepelie bounde unto yowe. And thus I beseeche god to sende unto your good Lordeshippe good and longe life and th encrease of moche honoure.

From my house in Bocton Malherbe the seconde of October 1576. Yowr most bounden.

Yf the L̃re be yet in your handes, I doo most humblie beseeche your good Lordeshippe to let mee have a Copie of it, and if it might conveniently be, I wold also be right gladde to knowe him that wrote it, which maie be easelie done if he be knowen and had that browght it.

The Medleys mentioned really were cousins of Thomas Wotton. His aunt Margaret married William Medley, and had two sons, William and Henry. She made a second marriage, with Thomas, fifth Marquess of Dorset, who did not treat his stepsons very nicely, as will be seen in No. XXXII, which shows that Wotton was Henry Medley's executor in 1582.

It will be noticed that the Earl of Leicester had sent his letter by a 'ryppier'; this word appears in the *Oxford Dictionary* as meaning one who brought fish from the coast.[1] Although there was no general postal system in 1576, there had been a Master of the Posts since 1516, who employed runners 'for the personal convenience of the sovereign and the individuals comprising the royal court'.[2]

XI. *Good councell geven to Edwarde Seymoure, Duke of Sommerset, one of the uncles of the late prince of most famous and blessed memorye King Edwarde the Sixt*

Take not all that you can, nor doo not all that you maye, for ther ys no greater daunger to a noble man then to let slyppe the Raynes of his Luste.

Let not Ambition entangle your mynde, for her nature ys to entangle her selfe. Let all untruthe be farre from you, that your thought be not hable to accuse your conscience. So use your Riches, as they be receyved into your howse, but not into your harte, for where covetousnes raynethe, ther vyce ys not long absent.

Beware that in all thinges that concerne your honour, personne, and substance, you put not fortune in trust, for the noble man that ys wyse wyll never hazarde the Daunger, weenyng to have remedye at her handes.

In straunge affayres go not to nyghe the bottome, and in your owne, doo not strayne nor enforce Tyme for demeanyng you so, for you maye remayne as you nowe be, or else you maye happe to remember what you were.

The daunger of noble men ys, that they cannot descende but fall, to the defence wherof nature ordeynethe the best frendes. Therfore percever in Amitye wythe suche as wyll rather staye you from falling, then set to their handes to helpe you up.

Be more carefull of conditions then of honoure, and doo well tyll you can doo no more, but never doo evell, thoughe you maye. Let not crueltye, but mercye and pittie overcome you for the Teares and complayntes of the wronged wyll come to Goddes

---

[1] The *English Dialect Dictionary* makes him carry his fish in a rip, or basket. Ray, in *South and East Country Words*, 1768, has: 'A pedder, dorser, or badger.'

[2] From Report of the Secret Committee of the House of Commons, 1844.

presence for your correction, and to the Kynges Eares for your disestimation.

In the offices that you bestowe have before your eyes rather the woorthye then your frendes, for among your frendes departe your Goodes, but not your conscience.

In that you councell be not affectionat; In that you discouncell be not passionat. In that you commande be not absolute, and in whatsoever you doo, be neyther too hastye nor disadvised, for the faultes be youres but the Judgement ys the worldes, and the greater the man ys, the more ys he noted.

Yf ye wyll not erre in your Councell, nor stumble in your Actes, nor fall from that you have, Then favoure hym that tellethe you the truthe, yea thoughe yt be Levened, and abhorre hym that tellethe you any untruthe, seeme yt never so pleasaunt, for yt ought rather to love hym that advisethe you nowe, then those that wyll make semblaunce to pyttie you hereafter.

Thomas Wotton's father, Sir Edward, was recalled from Calais to play some part, not a prominent one, in the weak case against the Duke which led to his imprisonment in 1549, and his execution on 22 January 1552.

  Few of those familiar with Somerset House remember that it preserves the name of this brother of Henry VIII's third Queen, Lady Jane Seymour, the mother of Edward VI. His building was replaced by the present one in 1775.

XII. *To the most honorable his very good Lorde, The Erle of Sussex, Lorde Chamberlayne of her Maties howse*

I knowe that your great favoure borne to my Sonne John Wotton, dyd in his first estate advaunce hym. I understande by the Letters of the right honorable my very good Lorde, the Lorde Cobham, that your great goodnesse latelye shewed hym, hathe from his imprisonment well delyvered hym. For these thinges and many other good thinges by your good Lordeshippe done unto hym, I doo bothe most humblie thanck you, and doo therfore thincke meeselfe deepely bounde unto you. Yf your good Lordeshippe shall at any tyme neede that that I maye doo, you shall fynde mee to doo yt in mynde faythfullye, in action redylye. And so I beseeche the Lorde to sende you in most honorable estate, a course of many joyfull yeres. From my howse in Saynte Mary's Craye, the xxvjth of Februarye 1578 Your most bounden.

Thomas Radcliffe, third Earl of Sussex, stands out as a successful Lord Deputy of Ireland in 1556 and Lord Lieutenant in 1562. In 1572 he was made Lord Chamberlain to the Queen. His continual opposition to Leicester is well drawn by Naunton, concluding with the warning against him which he gave when dying: 'You know not the beast as well as I do.'[1]

Wotton's second son John was born in 1550. Walton is not quite accurate in saying that he was knighted by the Queen, for he was knighted at Rouen by Robert, Earl of Essex, on 8 October 1591. Walton also says that the Queen intended him for preferment, 'but death in his younger years put a period to his growing hopes'. Actually his will was proved in 1597,[2] so that he lived to be forty-seven.

In an anthology called *England's Helicon*, 1600, are two pieces by John, who was not as good a poet as his half-brother Sir Henry; six lines will suffice:

> Jolly shepherd, shepherd on a hill,
>> On a hill so merrily
>> On a hill so cheerily,
> Fear not, shepherd, there to pipe thy fill,
> Fill every dale, fill every plain,
>> Both sing and say: 'Love feels no pain.'
>>>> *Damoetas' Jig in praise of his Love*

This is the first of several letters written from St. Mary Cray, where the manors of Saintlyng and Okemore had been owned by Sir Edward Belknap, whose daughter Anne married Sir Robert Wotton, grandfather of Thomas.[3]

---

[1] This Earl Thomas directed that a monument with effigies of his grandfather, father, and himself should be erected in a chapel attached to Boreham Church, Essex. The contract with the Dutchman Richard Steevens was amongst Peter Le Neve's papers, and has been quoted by numerous authorities from Weever, 1631, to Mrs. Esdaile, 1946. Though long neglected, and damaged, the monument still exists.

[2] Shaw's *Knights*, and *Archaeologia Cantiana*, vol. lviii, p. 22.

[3] Hasted, vol. i, p. 140.

XIII. *To the most honorable Sir Frauncis Walsingham knight, one of her Maties Principall Secretaryes*

Good sir, For the deliverye of my sonne John Wotton, depending principallye upon your great favoure signified unto mee by the Letters of the right honorable my very good Lorde, the Lorde Cobham, I doo most humblie and hartelye thancke you. Thus have you first delyvered mee (without good cause surely as I thincke, once shut up in prisonne), and nowe for my sake my sonne. And so in theese thinges and in all my other thinges (wherof some were of great weight), have I founde you so many wayes so good unto mee, as I assure you I knowe hym not in Englande unto whom I am so moche beholden. Yf my service maye at any tyme stande you instedde, you shall fynde mee to doo yt in minde faythfullye, in action redelye. And thus I beseeche the Lorde in honorable estate to sende you a course of many joyfull yeres. From my howse in Saynte Marye Craye the xxvj^{th} of Februarye 1578. Your most bounden.

Thomas's reference to his own imprisonment makes comment necessary. The official story is contained in two records of the Privy Council early in 1553 O.S.

> 21 January This daie Thomas Wotton esquier, for obstinate standing against matters of religion, was committed to the Fleete, to remayn a close prisoner.[1]
> 4 March. A lettre to the Wardeyn of the Fleete to permitt Mistres Wotton to repayre to hir husband so that she talke with hym in the presence of the Wardyn.[2]

The date of his release is not known.

Walton's story of the imprisonment is incredible. After saying that 'dreams are but a senseless paraphrase on our waking thoughts, or of the business of the day past', he goes on to say that Thomas's uncle the Dean, then an ambassador in France, dreamed for two nights in succession that Thomas was involved in a project which put his life in peril. After a good deal more about dreams he says that the Dean wrote to Queen Mary, and asked her to have Thomas examined by the lords of her Council 'in some such feigned questions as might give a colour for his commitment into a favourable prison'. When the Dean returned to

---

[1] *Acts of the Privy Council 1552–4*, p. 389.   [2] Ibid., p. 403.

England and visited his nephew in prison, Thomas admitted to him that 'he had more than an intimation of Wyat's intentions', and had held his tongue. Whether this was misprision of treason or not, he was certainly in the Fleet during the outbreak and suppression of the rebellion, and so escaped trouble when some of his Kentish friends lost their heads.

Our letter to Walsingham shows that he procured Thomas's release. We now know the excellence of Walsingham's secret service,[1] and it may well be that he heard of Thomas's friendship with Wyatt, and gave a hint to the Dean to act upon his knowledge. Twenty-five years after the event, Thomas considered he had been locked up 'without good cause surely, as I thincke'.

The failure of Wyatt's rebellion is now attributed to the lack of support in other counties promised by the Earl of Suffolk, Sir James Croft, and Sir Peter Cardew. There must have been a story about which was reported years later by Fuller, who says that Wyatt heard 'that one of his dear friends was cast into the Fleet (though for a cause unrelating to this plot, to which the party was privy)', and that he 'suspected, as guilt is ever jealous, that this his friend had betrayed the design, which made Wyatt anticipate the due date thereof'.[2] It may be only coincidence, but the particulars exactly agree with Thomas Wotton's case.

Another possible coincidence is that the date 1553 is deeply carved by a mason on the jamb of a fireplace in an upstairs room at Boughton Place. It is unlikely that the room was built at that date, which is certainly the year when Thomas was in grave danger, according to Old Style reckoning.

Walton chooses to give two more instances of Thomas's dreams. He says that a little before his death he dreamed that the University treasury at Oxford was being robbed by five persons, and that he wrote to his son Henry, then at Queen's College, about it. The letter was written in Kent and reached Oxford in three days, arriving on the morning following a robbery, and 'the five guilty persons were presently discovered and apprehended'. Anthony à Wood read this story and tried to verify it, but found no trace of any robbery at the time recorded anywhere.[3]

Another example of Walton's credulity about Thomas's supposed power of foreseeing the future will be found in the note to No. LIII.

---

[1] Many references occur to the fact that Walsingham spent his private fortune upon secret agents.

[2] *Church History*, bk. viii, sect. 1, § 25.

[3] *Athenae Oxonienses*, vol. ii, col. 644.

XIV. *To the right worshipfull his lovyng Cousyn Sir Henrye Cobham, Knight*

Sir, by your woordes spoken first to Edwarde Wotton and then to Sir Thomas Walsingham, I see that against reason you have towarde mee (for the matter in question betwene yo^u and mystres Flogge), conceyved some cause of unkyndenesse. What I have therin for her said unto you, you knowe, and what I have therin for you said unto her, shee knowethe. And seeyng bothe of you in that, I dyd for bothe of you with favorable affections towardes your selfes, mysconster my good meanyng (and out of a good meanyng I am sure for that purpose good woordes), to you bothe. I leave the matter to you, and your selfes to suche as you shall for that ende hereafter make choyse of, for surelye I mee selfe meane no more to meddle in yt. And so I beseeche the Lorde to sende you always right well to doo.

From Pykeryng howse in London the xvij^th of June 1577.

Your loving cousyn

Sir Henry Cobham became M.P. for the county in 1597, but he succeeded his father as eleventh Lord Cobham in the same year. Together with his younger brother George, he was involved in the Main Plot of July 1608, with which Raleigh was less directly associated. George was executed, but Henry saved his life by betraying all his friends.[1]

For Sir Thomas Walsingham see Letter LIII.

This and later letters are dated from Pickering House, which was not to be found in Cunningham and Wheatley's *London Past and Present*, &c. It was the home of Sir William Pickering (1516–75), and was on the east side of the highway in St. Mary Axe.[2] Pickering was both merchant and courtier, and was sent as resident Ambassador to France in 1551. He was successful, but becoming ill he asked to be recalled in 1553. He involved himself with the opponents of the Spanish marriage, and had to leave France, and remain in Italy and elsewhere, until his pardon was obtained by Dean Wotton. He then returned to England. He was

---

[1] His wife would have no more to do with him: *Complete Peerage* and Burke's *Extinct Peerage*. Carte calls Henry 'a worthless mortal, known to have neither honour nor virtue, principle, or veracity'. Weldon says that he was 'but one degree from a fool', edition 1650, p. 17.

[2] The editor is much indebted to Mr. P. E. Jones, Deputy Keeper of Guildhall Records, for identifying the site of Pickering House from Hustings Deeds.

certainly spoken of as an aspirant for the hand of Queen Elizabeth at one time.[1] His heiress was his natural daughter Hester, who married Thomas Wotton's son Edward, later made a peer. Their surviving son Thomas, second Lord Wotton, was baptized at St. Andrew Undershaft. There is a fine tomb in Great St. Helen's Church, which bears the recumbent effigy of Pickering. His library passed under his will to Hester's husband; his books were stamped with his arms, a chevron between 3 fleurs-de-lis.[2]

XV. *To his very loving cousyn Maximilian Brooke*

My good cousyn,

The dutye I owe unto your most honorable parentes dothe often tymes constrayne mee to repayre unto them. The love I am bounde to beare (and indeed beare), unto you dothe often tymes occasion mee wythe theym to common of you. The joye they have, the hope I have grounded upon the reaporte of your good inclination unto, and diligence in studye, dothe make theym as your parentes to love you deerely, dothe make mee as one of your frendes and meane kynsmen (and besyde mee a nomber of others), to esteeme you highelye. Of whiche thing to comforte you, and in the Trade you ar in to encourage you, I thought meete to wryte you a woorde or twayne.

That that you have well begonne you must in Studye well continue. Your parentes, your frendes, your countreye, all whiche have interest in you, look dulye for yt. The place where you be doth promyse yt, your selfe therby greatlye honored, shall hereafter blesse the tyme in whiche, and reverence the personnes by whiche you ar moved unto yt. Yf I doo not (as for lacke of learnyng to my great greefe I cannot), herein deale largelye and skylfullye, yet towarde you as a frende herein deale I faythfullye. And so I praye you take yt, for surelye so I meane yt. And in this sorte commending this matter unto you, I commende your selfe to the

[1] Letter from Duke of Saxony to Cecil, Oct. 1559, *Calendar of State Papers Foreign, 1559–1560*, p. 2.

[2] A Spanish translation of Petrarch's *Triumphs*, by Ant. de Obregon, 1541, is now in possession of Mr. Philip Hofer, of Cambridge, Mass. See Goldschmidt's *Gothic, etc., Bindings*, p. 293. Miss Miner, of Baltimore, is sincerely thanked for this information.

favoure of Almightie God. From Pykeryng howse in London, the xx[th] of June 1577.

Your very loving cousyn.

This letter was written to the eldest son of the tenth Lord Cobham, and brother of Henry mentioned in the last note. He was born on 4 December 1560, and there is a curious account of his christening 'in the Queene's closett . . . at the tyme of eveninge prayer'. Her Majesty was godmother, and the godfathers were William, Marquis of Northampton, and the Earl of Arundel.[1]

He followed this start in life by showing 'good abilities', and our letter implies it also. The poor fellow developed some disease, possibly pulmonary, for he was taken to Naples, and died in the hospital degli Incurabili of that city.[2] This premature death called forth a letter of condolence from Wotton, No. XLV, to his father, whose successor therefore was the unworthy Sir Henry Cobham, to whom No. XIV was written.

XVI. *To the right worshipfull his very loving frende Richard Payne Esquire*

Good sir,

Yt ys unto mee a matter of some greefe that a sute, and by sute a cause of unkyndnesse sholde contynue betweene your selfe of thone syde, and my Brother Whytton of thother syde. Where the thing in question ys of no great value, great pittye were yt that the recoverye wythe moche charge sholde be over deerely bought. And where the thing in question ys of no great value the losse (on which syde soever yt fall), in respecte of the thing yt selfe cannot be great. And where two honest and discreete gentlemen in sute meete together, the difficultye cannot be suche as that a fewe of their good frendes sholde not easelye see whiche of theym unto thother of theym dothe offer a poynt of wrong.

Supposing the thing in question to be of meane value, and knowing both of you to be very wyse and honest gentlemen, I thought

---

[1] *Archaeologia Cantiana*, vol. xii, p. 147, quoting Add. MSS. British Museum, 6113, f. 201.

[2] G. E. C. *Complete Peerage* and *Arch. Cant.*, vol. xii, p. 156, where 'during his absence abroad, he is said to have sent valuable information to Cecil'.

I might under theese termes by this meane comende unto you the ende of that matter. Whiche motion arysing from your frende, I praye you receyve in good parte. And so for your curtesye sondrie wayes shewed unto mee, acknowledging mee self to be moche bounde unto you, for this tyme I take my leave of you. From Pykeryng howse in London, the xxxth of Januarye, 1578.

Richard Payne was probably he who acquired Spelmonden, Horsmonden, from George Darell in 1568. He sold it in 1586, but this letter falls within the period of his ownership.[1]

'My brother Whytton' was the husband of Mary Finch, who was sister to Eleanor, the second wife of Thomas Wotton (Mrs. Morton). He lived at Lamberhurst, south-west of Tunbridge Wells, and only about three miles south of Horsmonden.

XVII. *To the right honorable his very good Lorde the Lord Burghley, lorde Treasaurer of Englande*

For your great goodnesse shewed to this poor gentleman Mr Arthure Barham, hymselfe speciallye, and in respecte of hym all his frendes generallye do thincke themselfes moche bounde unto you. Lefte for lyving in the lowest degree that I thincke the only sonne of any serjeaunt ever was, other recompence for so great a benefit as your great goodnesse hathe at this tyme shewed hym can he render none then this, that hymself and his shall contynuallye praye for you. In this plight standethe the case he hathe in hande. Peter Maplesdenne among other in the dayes of the late Queene was attaynted of Treason, she pardoned hym his lyfe, and by her Letters patentes in consideration of a good somme of moneye paid and to be paid, shee gave to hym and his heires the Landes he had. He dyethe, By whose deathe theese Landes came to his Childerne, Of theese Landes they sell unto Mr Serjeaunt Barham the best parte of that that they had, and a good parte of that that by his deathe his Sonne hathe. The question ys nowe whether from Peter Maplesdenne not restored in Bloudde, theese Landes in a course of discent maye fall to his childerne, ye or no. This question emong those that ar learned hathe bredde two

[1] Hasted, 1782, vol. ii, p. 386.

severall opinions, thone directlye against thother. The frendes of this yong gentleman advise hym for his owne commodities to take that waye that ys in title the surest, and for ende the shortest, that ys, that her Matie thoroughe the persuasion of your good Lordeshippe, and the payment of a reasonable somme of moneye, maye be pleased by waye of speciall remaynders in suche sorte to set over theese Landes unto hym, as his late father hathe done by his last wyll, whiche course (thoughe in limitation somewhat harde), wyll not I trust mislyke hym, when he shall remember that yt agreethe wythe his father's apparent meanyng, and when he shall knowe that yt proceedethe from one that this waye and every waye wyshethe his welldoyng. Upon whiche respectes I doo in that sorte humblie com̃ende yt unto you, and your selfe to the favoure of Amightie God.

From Pykeryng howse in London the

Humblie at the com̃aundement of your good Lordeshippe.

Arthur Barham appears to have been the son of Serjeant Nicholas Barham of Wadhurst,[1] who is named in *Ingoldsby Legends* as one of the guests at the House-warming in Bleeding Heart Yard. We are told there of

Queen's Serjeant Barham,
He lost, unless Sir Richard lies, his
Life at the famous Black Assizes.

The allusion is to Sir Richard Baker's *Chronicle*,[2] where the story is told of the Oxford Assizes in 1577, and the court was 'surprised by a pestilent savour', which killed the Lord Chief Baron Sir Robert Bell, the High Sheriff, Serjeant Barham, all the jurors, and 300 more.

Thomas Wotton's youngest son, the famous Sir Henry, went from Winchester to New College early in 1584. He was lodged in Hart Hall, and his 'chamber-fellow was Richard Baker his countryman, afterwards a knight and a noted writer'.[3]

As to Peter Maplesden, he looks like the grandson of one with both his names who lived at Lydd, and died in 1526, leaving a son Robert, the father of a Peter who may be the one attainted of treason in the time of Queen Mary.[4]

---

[1] Hasted, vol. ii, p. 290, noted.   [2] Printed in 1670, p. 375.
[3] Wood's *Athenae Oxonienses*, vol. ii, col. 643.
[4] Berry's *Genealogies*, p. 322.

XVIII. *To the right worshipfull his very lovyng frende Sir Thomas Kempe, knight*

Sir,

Betwene that that in respecte of privat affection I owe you speciallye, and that that towarde thexecution of Justice in respecte of a Christian man's dutye I owe to all men generallye, hathe rysen unto my mynde in manner of a conflicte, a matter of moche torment To execute suche processe upon you as ys in this Countye like to be procured against you, wyll be a matter heavye unto you, in respecte of you, yt wyll (as I have said), be very heavye unto mee. To suffer those persounes to lacke that remedye that the lawe justlye allowethe theym and straightlye tyethe mee to geve theym, maye be unto mee by waye of a fine, a matter of moche losse yt wyll be unto mee, (therfore greeved in conscience), as I have said, a matter of moche torment. Wythe theese two thinges I have first by Letter and afterwarde by mowthe, some what acquaynted Sir James Hales. Of suche as you seeme to be indebted unto, one Dalton, a Butcher of London, and Mr Andrewe Wyndesore, have ben wythe mee. The first in a lamentable maner declared the heavye plight he standethe in by the lacke of that that ye owe hym. The reason of the debt seemethe to be suche as every man wyll surely moche pittye hym. Thother saythe that his mother without interest freely lent you 100^li whiche shee hathe by her Testament assigned to be the portion and thonely portion of one of her daughters. For this somme and the charges bestowed about the recoverye of this somme, he demaundethe (I trowe), 140^li. I reckon surelye that theese personnes wolde be contented wythe some tracte of tyme to receyve their owne, so they might be assured to have yt. You ar (as a gentleman), in worshippe moche bounde to paye yt, you ar (as a Christian man), in conscience more bounde to paye yt. Yf ye thincke that upon any other respecte then suche as agreethe wythe thoffice of an honest man, I have said this unto you, you doo mee moche wrong. Iff in the seconde or thirde of the next monethe (about wch tyme I hope in god to be in my howse in Bocton), ye wyll sende Mr Mascall unto mee, I wyll then and there (God wylling), declare unto hym what course or state I reckon theese men in theese matters wolde wyllinglye stande upon. And this wythe my right hartie cõmendations for this tyme, I take my leave of you. From my howse in Saynte Marye Craye. the xvj[th] of Februarye 1578, Your very loving frende.

Sir Thomas Kempe was of Wye, north-east of Ashford. The most distinguished member of his family was the John Kempe who was Lord Chancellor in 1426, when he was Bishop of London, and again in 1450, when he was a Cardinal and Archbishop of York; two years later he was Archbishop of Canterbury. He founded a college of secular priests at Wye.

Sir Thomas was Sheriff in 1564-5, married successively the daughters of Sir Thomas Cheney and Sir Thomas Moyle, and had a daughter who married Sir James Hales (see No. XXX). He died in 1607.[1]

Presumably Wotton had been asked, as Sheriff, to authorize proceedings against 'his very loving frende'.

XIX. *To the right honorable Sir Frauncis Walsingham, Knight, one of her Ma[ties] principall Secretaryes*

Sir,

Certayne preachers in these partes properlye learned and towarde Christian religion well affected, and for their vertuous conditions well reaported, have a while in the market dayes at Cranebrooke used by turne to preache. This course in this thing can scarselye in any place in all this Countreye for place be done more fytlye, then in this Towne where the use or trade of good clothing dothe alwayes nouryshe a great nomber of yong people, and where the conveniencye and neccssitie of the market dothe once a weeke of all sortes and of all quarters moche encrease that nomber of people. And yf in other market Townes, bothe here and else where, the like maner of preaching by like good preachers were used, very likely ys yt that towarde thamendement of men's maners yt wolde be a matter of moche moment. Yf of theese men for this thing any complaint alredye be, or hereafter shalbe presented unto the right honorable our very good Lordes, the Lordes of her Ma[ties] most honorable preevye Councell, we doo then most humblie beseeche you that by your good meanes the veritye and weight of that complaint maye by our said right

_____
[1] Berry's *Genealogies*.

honorable Lordes theym selfes be examyned, yf their other busynesse of great importaunce maye well suffer yt. Or else that that complaint (yf any be), maye be hearde by suche Commissioners as in this Countye ar assigned for causes ecclesiasticall, and by theym, or the more parte of theym, a true reaporte in wryting of the veritie and weight of that complaint maye be made unto our said most honorable Lordes wherupon towarde the partyes accused yf they deserve yt maye insue just correction, or otherwyse for their honest doynges some good commendation. The necessarye use of this good thing dothe constrayne us, the good opinion we have conceyved of these men dothe move us, Your great goodnesse and curtesye do incourage us in this sorte to commende theym and this matter unto you. And so we commende yourselfe to the favoure of Almightie God.

Dated the thirde of Maye, 1579.

Cranbrook market was kept on Saturday, and was 'the greatest market in these parts' in 1659;[1] further it was 'formerly the centre of the clothing trade . . . carried on to a very considerable extent in the weald of Kent'.[2]

The provision of preachers at markets was the policy of the day. Henry, third Earl of Huntingdon, and President of the Council in the north, wrote on 27 June 1584:[3] 'I do all that I can to gett good preachers planted in the market townes of this country, in which somewhat is alreadie done.' The Earl died in 1595, 'having much wasted his estate by a lavish support of these hot-headed preachers', said Camden.

XX. *To the right honorable his very good Lorde the Lorde Aburgavennye*

My bounden dutye unto your good Lordeshippe most humblie remembered. I have delyvered unto your Solicitoure a note of 48 names towarde the making of suche a Jurye as sholde trye the matter in question betwene your good Lordeshippe and Mr Osbourne. And yf by bothe your consentes without sute in Lawe that question might have receyved an amiable and equall conclusion, yt had (I reckon), for bothe partes ben the best, and I

[1] Kilburne's *Topographie . . . of Kent*, p. 65.
[2] Mogg's *Paterson's Roads, 1829*, p. 15.   [3] Peck, *Desiderata Curiosa*, p. 151.

wolde for my parte surelye have ben right gladde of yt. Towarde this thing I have a little delt wythe Mr Osbourne, and in this thing (grounding still thassurance of his safetye upon the good rememberance of his owne woordes, wherof thoroughe the whole course of his lyfe he hathe alwayes had a great regarde), he speakethe yet of suche a waye as, measured by the rule of upright doyng, maye be done justlye, and in the doyng ys like to be done easelye, and being done wyll bryng unto your good Lordeshippe a matter of good commoditie. That that he hath herein said unto mee, I will (God willing), at Rochester on Thursdaye next declare eyther unto your selfe, or unto Sir Thomas Fane. The dutye I owe unto your good Lordeshippe holding mee self, I assure you sir, for your great curtesye many wayes moche bounde unto you. The long acquayntance I have had wythe, and the good will I beare unto Mr Osbourne (bothe of us in one howse and in one trade a good while, being brought up together), doo constrayne earnestlye to wyshe that eyther this waye, or any other good waye, this matter might without more a doo, fall to a small and frendlye ende.

And so I beseeche the Lorde in honorable estate to sende unto your good Lordeshippe a course of many joyfull yeres.

From Pykeryng howse in London, the xiij^th of June 1579. Humblie at the commandement of your good Lordeshippe.

The letter is written to Henry Nevill, sixth Lord Bergavenny, who was born 'after 1527', and, though twice married, left no male issue when he died on 10 February 1587. He was one of the peers at the trials of both Lady Jane Grey and Mary Queen of Scots.

The Mr. Osbourne with whom he had some difference of opinion may have been Robert Osborne, of Hartlip (1547–96), the son of John Osborne, auditor of the Exchequer, who died in 1577. Alternatively it might be Robert's brother John (1539–88).[1]

When Wotton says that he had been brought up with Osbourn 'in one trade', did he intend the earlier use of the word: 'a manner of life'? It appeared in the same sense in No. XV.

Sir Thomas Fane acquired Court Lodge, East Farleigh, and died in 1601.[2] An earlier owner was Sir John Baker, the grandfather of Sir Richard Baker, the Chronicler, who is mentioned in the note to No. XVII.

[1] Berry's *Genealogies*, p. 28. [2] Hasted, vol. ii, p. 145.

XXI. *To the right honorable my very good Lordes, the Lordes of her Maties most honorable Preevye Councell*

Our bounden dutyes unto your good Lordeshippes most humblie remembered. Meeting heere wythe Monsr Browbures, wee have by hym learned that little that he can tell us towarde the fynding of those persounes by whom he was heere of late lewdelye used.

And that that wee maye doo towarde thapprehension of theym, wyll wee assuredlye doo. And bycause wee shall in this matter have little occasion further to troble this bearer, wee have thought meete from hence to dispatche hym backe agayne.

And so wee beseeche the Lorde in most honorable estate to sende unto your good Lordeshippes a course of many joyfull yeres.

From Gravesende the xxv^th of Maye 1579.

Humblie at the comaundement of your good Lordeshippes,

XXII. *To the right honorable our very good Lordes the Lordes of her Maties most honorable Preevye Councell*

Our bounden dutyes unto your good Lordeshippes most humblie remembered, Yt maye please you to be advertised that by reason of theese assises meeting heere, and emong our selfes of sondrie thinges touching the good estate of this Countrye, commonyng heere together, wee thought yt wolde be unto her Matie a matter very honorable, and unto our neighboures of this Countreye a matter somewhat profitable, to transporte, into suche partes of beyonde the Sea as ar in good league and amitye wythe her said Matie, some good portion of those good thinges that the Lorde hathe in theese dayes most plentifullye blessed this Realme withall. The doyng or not doyng of whiche thing depending upon the advise of your good Lordeshippes, and the good pleasure of her said Matie, wee thought meete in humble sorte to present unto your grave consideration. Honorable unto her Matie (wee reckon), yt must needes be, that other Realmes shall from this Realme receyve the use of suche good thinges as wee maye well spare. Profitable unto the people of this Realme wyll yt assuredlye be there to sell theym where at convenient Rates they maye have redye moneye for theym. And the reaporte of this generall permission (as wee thincke fyt for the tyme present), ys in respecte of the tyme to come at the least like to bryng this benefit, that the people hoping still to fynde some one place or other where they maye at good pryces utter the frutes of their travayle, wyll still contynue that good course of Tyllage that they ar nowe in, whiche in our opinion was in matter or quantitie of doyng never done so largelye, nor in fourme or maner of doyng never done so orderlye.

And howe meete that thing ys for a good parte of the soyle of the Realme, and howe necessarye the contynuance of that thing ys for all the people of the Realme (that shall this waye about a good thing be well occupyed), wee referre to the grave consideration of your good Lordeshippes.

Yf wee have herein erred, the desire to doo our Countreye good hathe ben the cause. Upon whiche respecte wee doo most humblie beseeche you in good parte to receyve that that herein wee have done.

And so wee beseeche the Lorde in most honorable estate to sende unto your good Lordeshippes a course of many joyfull yeres. From Maydeston the xxiiij[th] of Julye 1579

Humblie at the comaundement of your good Lordeshippes.

This letter was written at the Assizes, which had begun on the previous day, 23 July.

The Privy Council's reply was dated 27 July, and cited the statute of 13 Elizabeth (1571), with the closing proviso: 'nevertheles haveing regarde that according to the other branchs of the statute the same be staied in time, if thereby any want or dearth shall ensue'.[1]

The year 1578 had also yielded a good harvest and Wotton had written to Lord Burleigh on 15 October 1578, supporting a licence to Doctor Hector to export 200 quarters of wheat 'to parts beyond the sea'.[2] That letter closely resembles the present one, but a glance at the schedule of letters (p. xx) will show that no letters were copied in the book during 1578 N.S.

[1] *Acts of the Privy Council 1578–1580*, p. 208.
[2] *Hist. MSS. Commission Report*, Hatfield, series 9, pt. 2, p. 216.

Twenty-five years later, the Act of 1 Jac. C. 25, allowed the export of corn 'at certaine prices, and the same to bee restrained againe by the King's Proclamation'.

XXIII. *To his very loving cousyn Mr Henry Cheyney, at Brodegates in Oxenforde*

Yf where ye wolde and sholde cure, (for lacke of Skyll), ye kyll,— towarde the partys that sufferethe yt—remedye ys ther none. By the partye that dothe yt (howe great soever he be), just recompencé can be made none. The untimely practice of Lawyers and Phisitians seemethe to be the cause that this Realme hathe fewe good Lawyers and fewer good Phisitians.

Yf ye will towarde the benefit of your patient comfortablye, for your selfe towarde the worlde commendablye, as a good Christian man towarde the Lorde dutifullye, take in hande the office of a good phisitian, yt ys not ynoughe that ye seeme so to be, unlesse that in deede so ye be; and that can ye not be without moche Studye, nor by studye moche knowledge can ye not have, without moche tyme and moche payne. And so consequentlye in myne opinion by this hastye course forsaking your studye ye hurte your selfe moche, and those that ye shall deale withall ye ar like to hurte more. When I thincke that emong a manye of learned men ӯt ar in Oxenforde, I thincke that I neede not thus to wryte. When I thinke what I ought herein to doo, I am mee thinckethe still bounde to wryte yt. This notwithstanding I have unto this bearer delyvered xxv^s. And so I wyshe you alwayes well to doo. From Pykeryng howse in London, the xvij^th of July, 1579. Your loving frende

With some hesitation it is suggested that the young man to whom this letter was written may have been the son of the Rev. Henry Cheney whom Wotton had presented to the rectory of Ringwould on 7 November 1569.[1] Ringwould is nearly mid-way between Deal and Dover, and came to the Wottons when Sir Robert married the Belknap heiress. It may well be that the Rev. Henry was connected in some way with Sir

---

[1] Hasted, vol. iv, p. 178. The next presentment was on 2 May 1578, so the Rev. Henry may have been dead when Wotton wrote.

Thomas Cheney, Treasurer of the Household to Edward VI, and Lord Warden of the Cinque Ports. He died in 1558, and his son Henry became 'the extravagant Lord Cheney', rebuilding his house at Shurland, and entertaining the Queen there in 1563 and 1576. He sold the Kentish property, and died at Toddington, Beds., in 1587.

Inquiry was made of the Bursar of Pembroke College, and Mr. G. R. F. Bredin was so very kind as to write as follows: 'Our records of Broadgate Hall, on which Pembroke was founded in 1624, are not very complete [until after 1578]. I notice a footnote to the 1578 page which says that Thomas Barfote was servant of Mr. Cheney, privilegiatus. This would indicate that Cheney was then in residence, and had probably matriculated two or three years before. Thomas Barfote had probably been accepted as a student in a humble capacity, so that he could serve Mr. Cheney.'

The Librarian of the Royal College of Physicians was good enough to make a search, and can find no record of any Henry Cheney at this date.

Wotton's phrase, 'by this hastye course forsaking your studye ye hurte your selfe moche', suggests that he knew Henry was not doing his best to qualify himself. It is a kindly letter, and the gift which accompanied it was clearly meant to encourage a young man who may have felt himself unfitted for the vocation of medicine.

XXIV. *To the right honorable his very good Lorde Therle of Leycester*

My goode Lorde, Right sorye am I that in any person in this Countie towardes her Maties service any suche default sholde be founde, as wherof your good Lordeshippe, or any other Bodye, sholde have cause to complayne. I have by my Letters commended unto my Masters the Justicers of the peace, upon other occasions nowe assembled at Rochester, the delyverye of that proportion of Otes that ys yet behynde. I trust they wyll here upon wth speede cause theym to be sent in. I have also required theym that the next Sessions maye be the tyme in whiche, and Maydestone the place at whiche, wee maye in an indifferent sorte divide the 700 quarters of Otes into suche Limites within this countye, as out of wch they sholde hereafter be yerely yelded towarde the furniture of her Maties Stable. By this Letter neverthelesse I nowe doo as by mowthe lately I dyd, make this humble petition unto you, that this Countie maye be (yf by that treatie that you have wythe other Counties thoroughe the good pleasure of your good Lordeshippe yt maye convenientlye be), rated at 600 quarters.

The resolution and graunt of wch poynt must proceede from that favoure that I hope you beare towarde this Countie. And so (with the rememberaunce of my most bounden dutie), I beseeche the Lorde in most honorable estate to sende you a course of many joyfull yeres.

From my howse in Bocton Malherbe the xviijth of Marche, 1578.

The Earl of Leicester at this date was Master of the Horse, and the purveyance of oats for the Royal stable was under his control.

It will be seen from the next item that Wotton wrote to twenty-eight 'justicers' in Kent, calling for a better allocation of the quota demanded from Kent.

XXV. *To the right worshipfull his very loving frendes*

Sir Henry Cobham
Sir Thomas Walsingham } knightes 1

Walter Roberts Esquire 4

Sir Thomas Cotton
Sir Christopher Alleyne } knightes
Sir Thomas Fane

George Moulton
Robert Rychers } esquires
Robert Byng
} 2

John Cobham
William Crowmer
George Fynche } esquires 5
George Clyfforde

Sir James Hales knight

Edwarde Boyes
Richarde Hardres
John Fyneux
John Boyes
Thomas Palmer } esquires 3
William Partheriche
Thomas Hales
William Hammon

John Lennarde
Thomas Wylloughbye
Raphe Bossvile } esquires 6
Thomas Potter

Thomas Coppinger Esquire 7
Roger Twysdenne Esquire 8

Yt ys (I thincke), by this tyme unto all my Masters the Justicers of the peace of this Countie right well knowne that towarde the mayntenaunce of her Maties Stable, the right honorable Therle of Leycester ys well pleased from hence to have yerelye in Otes 700 Quarters, and moe he meanethe not to charge this countye wythe. Upon howe many severall Limetes this quantitie, (and upon every suche Limete howe moche of this quantitie), of Otes shall be layed, ys a thing emong us yet undetermyned.

The resolution wherof requirethe a meeting and conference of all, or the most parte of all my said Masters the Justicers of the peace. This meeting maye be (yf the Lorde suffer yt and you shall thincke yt meete so to be), in Maydestone at the next quarter Sessions holden there. Towarde a conclusion wythe the said right honorable Erle in the matter of theese Otes, I coulde at London doo no more then I dyd. And towarde the proportionyng of theym into sondrie Limetes (which by the quantitie and qualitie of the Limete ought to be done equallye, and wythe expedition speedelye), I can doo no more then nowe I doo. Yf those Otes shall not be delyvered, wherof inclosed in my Letter I sent a note unto my masters latelye assembled at Rochester, a great fault (I feare) wyll be therfore layed upon us all.

Yf out of your Limete therfore any of those Otes ought to be had, I beseeche you so deale wythe your Constables as they may be dulye delyvered. Maydestone ys the place at whiche, the xxiij[th] of this present ys the daye in which they ought to be delyvered. And thus for this tyme wythe my right hartie comendacons, I take my leave of you.

From my howse in Bocton Malherbe the viij[th] of Aprill 1579.

The word 'Limete' [limit] in this letter, which was sent to twenty-eight Justices of the Peace, presumably bears the meaning: 'a region defined by a boundary' (*Shorter Oxford Dictionary*), but the names, so carefully set out in eight numbered categories, are not related to the 'five laths and severall divisions of Justices to the peace' given by Kilburne. Group 3 alone cover the whole county, as the following six names show:

Name	Of	Lath
William Hammon	Crayford, Dartford	Sutton at Hone
William Partheriche	Merton, Rochester	Aylesford
John Boyes	Bonnington, Ashford	Shipway
Edward Boyes	Nonnington, Sandwich	St. Augustine
Richard Hardres	Upper Hardres, Hythe	,, ,,
Thomas Hales	Horden, Tenterden	Scray

The eight groups have no territorial basis, therefore.

XXVI. *To the right honorable his very good Lorde the L. Cobham, L. Wardenne of the fyve Portes*

Yt ys to a great manye very well knowne that Clyffesende ys within the Libertie of my manoure of Sheryvesende; y^{t} ys to mee well knowne (emong whiche I thincke Cole hymselfe ys one), that bothe theese Shippes fell within Clyffesende. And I have hearde that from thence, wythe moche laboure and good charge, they were haled into the Haven of Sandwyche. Yf none of theym bothe fell there, of none of theym bothe under the title of groundage by right I ought to have nothing. And of none of theym (and of no other besyde theym), by wrong I meane not to clayme or get any thing. I have hereupon by Letter intreated my frend and fermoure Mr Gawnt, in an assured sorte to enquire the veritie of the poynt. And yf he fynde that none of theym fell within Clyffesende to redelyver unto — Cole your servaunt the somme of v^{li} by the said — Cole lately taken unto hym. And yf he fynde that bothe the Shippes fell there, I have also requyred hym to delyver unto your said servaunt the said somme of v^{li}. The losse of the whole (wch I ought to have said), shall (in respecte of the thing yt selfe being the whole), little greeve mee. The losse of the halfe (wch I had delyvered in the steade of the whole wch I ought to have had) shall (in respecte of the thing yt selfe being but the halfe), lesse greeve mee. But wythe yt thus moche I saie, howe I dyd little looke that from your good Lordeshippe any suche poynt of injurye sholde in suche sorte be offered unto mee, as besyde your selfe a nomber of other must needes knowe yt, and heare of yt. And I thought that I might well the lesse looke for yt, when I had your owne Letter as an assurance or wytnesse, that unto mee yt sholde not be offered. And yf the Lorde of Lordes had somewhat altered the case, and for place had set me where you ar, and you where I am (the rest of the thinges on eche syde mutuallye standing still betwene us as they doo), I wolde at no tyme in any matter have used that course towarde you that your good Lordeshippe hathe at this tyme in this matter used towarde mee. And so in humble sorte I take my leave of you, from Pykering howse in London this Saturdaye the xxiijth of Aprill 1580.

William Brooke, tenth Lord Cobham, was born in 1527, and was made Lord Warden of the Cinque Ports in 1558. Queen Elizabeth visited him during her Progress in 1559, and again in 1573, when she visited Wotton. He served on embassies in 1578 and 1588, and died on 6 March 1597.[1]

Wotton was a kinsman and close friend of Lord Cobham, as Nos. XV, XXXV, and XLV show, and this letter calls Lord Cobham's attention to an apparent error of his agent Cole. Groundage was a duty levied on vessels which lay on a shore or beach (*O.E.D.*), and Cole had paid for one when two had come aground.

Wotton's 'manoure of Sheryvesende' is Hasted's Sheriff's Court,[2] and is in the hamlet of Hoo and the parish of Minster. In 1365 it had belonged to Robert Corby, and passed to the Wottons when the Lord Mayor Sir Nicholas married Joan Corby.[3]

XXVII. *To the right worshipfull his very loving Cousyn Leonarde Dannet, Esquyre*

Right sorie wolde I be that betwene us two (in nature neere Kynsmen, by nombre of yeres nowe olde men), and suche thinge sholde arise as sholde be moche unfyt for every of us in age considered by hym selfe severallye, more unfyt for bothe of us in nature considered together joyntlye. The thing that ye deteyne from mee ys a parte of that that by graunt ye conveyed unto my late good uncle. Unto this thing I doo moche desire that without sute, in a quyet sorte, I maye be agayne restored. And hereunto I praye you about the myddle of the next terme let me have your reasonable answer.

And thus wythe my right hartie commendacons for this tyme I take my leave of you. From Pykering howse in London this Sondaye the first of Maye 1580.

Your very loving cousyn.

[1] William Harrison, author of the famous Description of England for Holinshed' *Chronicle*, 1577, had been domestic chaplain to this Lord Cobham, and dedicated his useful work to him.

[2] Hasted thought it might be named after a notable sheriff of the late twelfth century, but Kilburne cites Thorne's chronicle of the eighth-century nunnery on this spot, in which it is called Surreve's Hope (p. 193). 'Hope' was an anchorage in the river Wantsume, or Stour, which then ran by the place.

[3] Hasted, vol. iv, pp. 321–2.

The younger of Thomas Wotton's two brothers was William, who had married Mary, daughter of John Dannet; they left no children.[1] The relationship of Leonard to John has not been traced, but it made him one of Thomas's numerous 'very loving Cousins'. However, Thomas is writing as heir of his uncle the Dean, and is claiming in that capacity.

A note upon the Dean will be found at No. LII.

XXVIII. *To the right worshipfull his very loving frende S*[r] *John Ryvers, knight*

I understande from my cousyn Frauncis Thynne that towarde the payment of the debt he owethe you, he ys well contented by good assuraunce yerely to paye you xxx[li]. Let mee intreate you (good Sir) at his handes in this sorte to take your owne, moche losse this course cannot bring unto you,—restored unto libertie, moche comforte ys yt like to bring unto hym. He denyethe that he hathe in any sorte sought to deceyve you. Yf he sholde so doo, I am for my parte right sorye for yt, and he ought for his parte bothe to confesse yt, and moche to be asshamed of yt. But yf the rememberaunce of that poynt (without losse towarde you by like well passed), sholde occasion you still to contynue the course of his imprisonement, the correction in myne opinion ys greater then ys fyt, for the partes of his offence. And in this tyme howe farre suche a purpose ought to be from the mynde of suche a one as ys in profession a christian man, in yeres an olde man, in estate thoroughe the providence of God a ryche man, I doo most hartelye and earnestlye intreate you to consider. Yf you shall wythe a pure mynde be good unto hym, the Lorde of his mercye will therfore rewarde you, hym selfe and his frendes (emong w[ch] I am one), shall therfore thincke theym selfes moche bounde unto you. Under whiche termes I commende hym and this matter unto you, and your selfe to the favoure of almightie God. From Pykering howse in London, this Sundaye, the viij[th] of Maye 1580
Your very loving frende.

Sir John Rivers was the son of Richard, who was steward to Edward Stafford, Duke of Buckingham. Sir John was Lord Mayor in 1578, and owned Chafford, at the south end of Penshurst parish, in 1576. The

---

[1] Burke's *Extinct Peerage*, p. 593.

family continued there until 1743, when the property went to the Rev. Sir Peter Rivers, who married Miss Gay, the Bath heiress, and took the name of Rivers-Gay.[1]

Today the creditor is less interesting than the debtor. Francis Thynne 'from his infancy had an ingenuous inclination to the study of Antiquity, and especially of Pedigrees. Herein he made such proficiency that he was preferred, towards the end of the Raign of Queen Elizabeth to be Herald, by the title of Lancaster'.[2]

From Tonbridge School he went to Magdalen College, Oxford, and was later member of Lincoln's Inn. Wood gives the titles of many papers by Thynne.[3] Some were included in later editions of Holinshed and there are eight in the complete edition of Hearne's *Collection of Curious Discourses*, 1773.

XXIX. *To the right worshipfull his very assured loving frende Edward Waterhouse Esquire*

Thamendement of the poor estate that my Brother Vyncent Fynche stoode in (next the providence of almightie God depending cheefelye upon your good favoure), hathe deepely bounde hym unto you. The reaporte of yt here emong his frendes (wherof I am as I am bounde to be, one), hathe also moche bounde mee unto you.

Yf in respecte of this yt shall rest in mee any wayes to stande you in steadde, you shall in a faythfull sorte here upon fynde mee redye to doo yt. For the state of my Bodye being an olde man, meete to be farre from the Courte, for the disposition of my mynde bent to be a Countrey man, unfyt for the causes of the Courte, I cannot and therfore I doo not wryte you any newes.

And this wythe my right hartie commendations to your selfe, and by your mowthe to my good frende and neighboure Sir Warham Sentleger, for this tyme I take my leave of you.

From Pykering howse in London, this fridaye the viij[th] of Maye 1580.

[1] Hasted, vol. i, p. 417, and later sources.
[2] Fuller's *Worthies*, 1811, vol. i, p. 508, where he is said to have aided Holinshed.
[3] *Athenae*, vol. ii, cols. 107–11.

Edward Waterhouse was one of the Irish Council, and was knighted soon after this letter was written. He is buried at Woodchurch, some ten miles west of Ashford, in 1591.[1]

Vincent Finch was brother of Erasmus (No. XXXVII) and of Eleanor, whom Wotton married when he was a widower and she was widow of Robert Morton.

Sir Warham St. Leger's mother was daughter of Hugh Warham, and niece of Archbishop William Warham. He was knighted in 1565, and was made Governor of Munster. His first wife Ursula was the daughter of the fifth Lord Bergavenny.

The St. Legers lived at Ulcombe, only a few miles west of Boughton Malherbe, but Sir Warham's son William sold the Ulcombe property, and settled in Ireland. His grandson became Viscount Doneraile of the first creation.

This letter is dated Friday, 8 May, and the previous letter was dated Sunday, 8 May. The latter was correct in 1580.

XXX. *To the right worshipfull his very loving frende Sir James Hales, knight*

Your Letter of the xxx[th] of Julye was late yester night by one of my folkes here delyvered unto mee, and unto his handes (as he said), that daye by a woman unknowen here delyvered unto hym.

Yf you will well consider that that I wrote unto you, cause of greefe have I offered you none. A reaporte (by like) was made unto you, that M[r] Councell sholde saye that hee relyed hym selfe moche upon mee. Of this reaporte (reteynyng still to yourselfe the name of the reaporter), at Maydestone you made mee acquaynted. I praye you, good sir, indifferentlye consider whether in the presence of those gentlemen (whose names I sent you), I might not in that place more fytlye tell M[r] Councell of that reaporte openlye; then therein deale wythe hym secreatelye.

Let the case be that emong theese gentlemen your selfe had ben one, and that they had ben (as I thincke all of theym were), your very good frendes, and most of theym acquaynted wythe the veredicte that betwene your vertuous mother and Mr Councell there lately passed, and unto some of theym this poynt also right

[1] *Arch. Cant.*, vol. xiv, p. 350.

well knowne, that he had somtyme ben a servaunt unto my late good father. Yf nowe, out of your and their companye you and they sholde have seene mee to have gone unto hym, and in se-create sorte to have delt wythe hym, howesoever you and they wolde have taken yt, I sholde surelye have done full yll in yt. And yf in your and their presence I might not well have done yt, by your absence the case ys little altered. Qui vadit plane, vadit sane. And in this poynt ys the substance of the offence, whiche maye be placed emong suche as ar rather taken then geven. And yf without cause ye seeke this waye to make mee a straunger unto you, the faulte ys youres, and not myne. And hereof I dare make the deerest frende you have lyving the Judge. And thus (passing over that that against Mr Councell I dyd for your vertuous mother), I beseeche the Lorde in good estate to sende you a course of many joyfull yeres. From my howse in Bocton Mal-herbe the IXth of August 1580. Your very loving frende.

Sir James Hales, of the Dongeon, Canterbury, was knighted in 1572. He married Alice, daughter of Sir Thomas Kempe (see No. XVII). In 1589 he was appointed treasurer of an expedition under Sir John Norris ('General Norreys'); this was sent according to a trading agree-ment with Portugal, which had been seized by Spain, and the English agreed to garrison some forts in Portugal. A large proportion of the troops was untrained, and the 200 ships used sailed before they were ready, or victualled. The expedition was a failure, and the losses were appalling.[1] On his way home Sir James Hales died at sea, and was dropped overboard in full armour, except that his head was bare. This is represented on his monument on the north side of the nave in Canterbury Cathedral.

Underneath is painted a scene which recalls the death of Sir James's grandfather of the same names. He was made a Justice of the Common Pleas in 1549, and sat in the Court which deprived Bishop Gardiner in 1551. Although a strong Protestant, he alone of the judges opposed the proclamation of Lady Jane Grey. Later he gave offence by some remarks which he made at the Kent Assizes; Queen Mary forgave him for this and reappointed him as judge. When he went to take the official oath, it was before Gardiner, and the revengeful prelate refused him, and even committed him to prison for some months. This disturbed his mind and he attempted suicide with a knife, but was rescued and

---

[1] *Cambridge Modern History*, vol. iii, p. 317.

released. He went to stay with his nephew, son of his brother Thomas of Thannington, and threw himself into the river Stour, near the City boundary, and was drowned. The painting shows Thannington Church and the river.[1]

The fifth in descent from the Judge, by his younger son Edward, was a baronet who married one of the three daughters of the second Lord Wotton. Whilst still very young and inexperienced he was persuaded by a hare-brained friend to involve himself in a desperate attempt to save the royal cause in 1648. It led to his flight to the Continent and he never returned, dying in France after the Restoration.[2]

XXXI. *To his verye assured frende Mr Best*

Of all the deere that ever you had, I sende you (I feare) the woorst, and yet of all those that I nowe have I sende you (I thincke) the best. But seeyng hee ys neyther suche as you deserve, nor suche as for you I desyre hee sholde bee, in the place of this I praye you, appoynt when and where ye will have suche as my Parke can geve, when yt can geve best, for suche hathe your curtesye ben towarde mee, as at my handes yt deservethe greater matter then Buckes.

And so unto your Daughter in her maryage I wyshe great joye, and unto your selfe by her maryage great comforte.

From my howse in Bocton Malherbe the xxjth of Maye 1580. Your very assured frende.

There was a Richard Best, of Bibrook in Kennington, near Ashford, who had a son John, born in 1573.[3]

Mr. Best may have belonged to the family of which a much later member, Thomas son of Mawdisley Best of Boxley, acquired Chilston Park and rebuilt the house in the mid-eighteenth century.[4]

[1] The monument is in Cowper's *Monumental Inscriptions of Canterbury*, 1897. The notes on the Judge are largely taken from Foss's *Biographical Dictionary of Judges*, 1870, p. 328. Dr. W. Urry is sincerely thanked for calling attention to this unusual memorial.

[2] The story is told at length, and most brilliantly, in Book XI of Clarendon's *History of the Rebellion*. It deserves to be read in full and does not belong to these pages.

[3] *Visitation of Kent 1594*, ed. Ralph Griffin, p. 4.

[4] Hasted, vol. ii, p. 435.

In the church of Boughton Malherbe are many memorials to the Best family, of the eighteenth and early nineteenth centuries.

XXXII. *To the right worshipfull his very loving Cousyns James Morice and William Medleye Esquires*

In thadministration of the Goodes of my cousyn Henrye Medleye as one of his executoures, I have not heretofore medled, nor meane not hereafter in any sorte to meddle. Being in nature unto his Childerne a kynsman, and in devotion a frende, I fynde mee selfe bound to doo (and for theym wolde I be right gladde to doo), whatsoever I might convenientlye doo.

Right sorye am I that the Lorde Thomas as their neere kynsman wyll not in such sorte love theym, or, beholding the meane estate they stande in, wyll not in such sorte pitie theym, as that hee wyll quyetlye suffer theym to injoye that that by their good father was lefte unto theym.

Towarde the resolution of the question, as a Lawyer I can saye nothing, for a thing of suche a value as ys mentioned in your Letter, the somme offered to be paid ys little, the maner of the payment dothe make yt lesse. A daungerous thing ys yt, for personnes so meane as the Childerne of my Cousyn Henrye Medleye ar, against a personage in lyving so great as the Lord Thomas ys, to commyt to the discretion of a Jurye the Validitie of the Lease, depending upon the intention of theym that made yt. And therfore yf his Lordeshippe wolde from one thousande markes aryse to a thousande pounde, to be paid to theym, and the survivoure of theym, I wolde for my parte (as their Kynsman and not as an Executoure to their father), wyshe theym rather wythe the losse of the Lease to take yt, then by sute (subjecte to great trouble and charge), to stande in the defence of that, that an undiscreete or a partiall Jurye maye soone overthrowe. The case ys in value somewhat weightie, in title somewhat doubtfull. I cannot by Letter in this tyme saye more unto yt then this, that ys that your selfe and my Cousyn William Medleye of all other can best tell what ys herein to be done. And so wythe my right hartie commendaĉons for this tyme, take my leave of you. From my

howse in Bocton Malherbe this Weddensdaye the xj[th] of Julye
1582.

Your very loving Cousyn.

The note to No. X has already explained that Henry and William
Medley were really cousins german of Thomas Wotton. Their mother
took as her second husband Thomas Sackville, who was created Baron
Buckhurst in 1567, and is Wotton's 'the Lorde Thomas'; he was created
Earl of Dorset in 1603. He was evidently unsatisfactory as a stepfather.

The only James Morice of this date seems to be a trustee, together
with Thomas Gawdye, for the manor of Gravesend. This was in 1581.
They held it only a short time, for two years later it was vested in Lord
Cobham.[1]

XXXIII. *To the right worshipfull his very loving frende George Morton Esquire*

Howe the state of your lyving maye maynteyne the charges that
your abode in London dothe put you unto, How your abode
there without cause dothe answer the dutie ye owe unto your
vertuous wyfe and Childerne (as farre as I see lefte to theym selfes
in the Countreye), everye man maye easelye judge. Of theese two
thinges meete yt ys you sholde have, and I doo desire you that
without delaye ye wyll have a deepe and dutifull consideration.
And thus for this tyme in hast I take my leave of you. From my
howse in Bocton Malherbe this Weddensdaye the XXVth of Julye
1582.

This is the first of several letters to Wotton's own stepson. Walton says
that Thomas was urged by friends to make a second marriage, and
replied that he would not marry one who had children, or a lawsuit, or
was of his kindred. Then Walton adds that Thomas did marry one 'in
whom were a concurrence of all those accidents against which he had
so seriously resolved'. His good taste leaves it there; he may have known
that the stepson was troublesome, or his informant, Sir Henry Wotton,
may have been reticent about the shortcomings of his half-brother.

When Sir Henry went to Venice as ambassador he took with him
Albertus Morton, son of George Morton of Eshere Chilham. Albertus

[1] Hasted, 1778, vol. i, p. 448, citing the Escheat Rolls of 23 Eliz., part 5.

was first cousin once removed of Sir Henry, but was called nephew by him. Albertus was knighted and made Secretary of State in 1625, and, when he died, Sir Henry wrote 'Tears at the grave of Sir Albertus Morton', which Walton printed. The lines which Sir Henry wrote on his widow are more familiar to all:

> He first deceas'd; she for a little tri'd
> To live without him; lik'd it not, and di'd.

XXXIV. *To the right honorable the Lordes of her Ma$^{tie's}$ most honorable Preevye Councell*

Wee doo most humblie beseeche your good Lordeshippes to geve us leave to make this humble petition unto you. That where the Deane and Chapter of Christeschurche in Canterburye ar bounde yerelye (as wee thincke in pios usus), to bestowe the somme of one hundred poundes. Yt maye like you by your favourable Letters to requyre theym of this somme to bestowe upon Mystres Storer some convenyent yerelye portion. The husbonde of this woman not long agone dyed here, and a long tyme lyved here, in his doyng towarde all men very vertuouslye, in his preaching unto a nomber of men, bothe christianlye and lernedlye. By his deathe this woman ys nowe a wydowe, and in estate a poore wydowe, and yet surelye still a very honest Bodye. And so cannot the said Deane and Chapter of the said somme of one hundred poundes to so good a purpose well appoynted, geve any portion to any other person that for demeanure shall better deserve yt, or for estate afore this woman shall have more neede of yt. Your good lordeshippes shall herein binde her perpetuallye to praye for you.

Wee shall in her behalfe herein accompt our selfes deepelye bounde unto you. The Lorde of heaven and earthe for this and a nomber other of your most noble actions shall in earthe here blesse you, and in heaven hereafter of his mercye rewarde you. Dated in Maydeston the Tenthe of September 1582 Humblie at the commandement of your good Lordeshippes.

This most characteristic letter of Wotton's on behalf of the widow of a parson was written from Maidstone, possibly at Quarter Sessions, when the signature of Kentish 'justicers' could be added to his own, as the 'wee' indicates.

The deceased Mr. Storer is mentioned on the last page of the original church register of Staplehurst, in this way:[1] 'Mr Storer, the precher of the Towne of Maydestone, preched April 20 and August 31. 1578.'

XXXV. *To the right honorable his very good lorde the Lorde Cobham, Lorde Warden of the fyve portes*

For the honorable curtesye and great good cheere latelye re-ceyved at the handes of your good Lordeshippe, I doo most humblie and hartelye thancke you.

Yf yt shall rest in mee any waye to stande you in stedde, you shall in a faythfull sorte fynde mee redye to doo yt. I doo most humblie beseeche you, sir, wythe yourselfe a little to consider the motion I made unto you in the behalfe of the Lorde Cheefe Baron. Yf eche of you be (as eche of you unto eche other of you seeme to be), professed ennemyes, in respecte of your being here in earthe (whiche cannot be long), yll yt ys unto you bothe; in respecte of your being out of the earthe (whiche without ende must have a course of contynuance), woorse yt ys unto you bothe.

Yf in stedde of your woonted familiaritie ther be nowe betwene you (your myndes not offended), nothing but a strangenes, that may be soone reformed. And surelye that offence and injurye ought to be great, the rememberaunce wherof sholde in the brest of any person, have a perpetuall place. And yf suche a thing be meete to be removed, the sooner yt ys done, the better ys yt done. And of bothe sydes most woorthye of prayse and honoure ys hee by whom yt ys thus done. This hee saythe that for your estates dothe honoure you bothe, that for his mynde dothe love you bothe, that for poyntes of singuler curtesye dothe accompt hym selfe moche bounde to you bothe.

And so I beseeche the Lorde in honorable estate to sende you a course of manye joyfull yeres.

From my howse in Bocton Malherbe this Sondaye the xvj^th of September 1582.

Humblie at the commandement of your good Lordeshippe.

---

[1] *Archaeologia Cantiana*, vol. xxviii, p. 293.

Sir Roger Manwood, the Lord Chief Baron of this letter, had a character in which good and evil were so mixed that Lord Cobham may easily have seen some of the more ugly traits, and Wotton began to do so later, see No. XLIII.

XXXVI. *To the right honorable our very good Lorde the Earle of Warwicke*

Our bounden dutyes unto your good Lordeshippe most humblie remembered. Right sorye ar wee that the lewde demeanure of Thomas Wandenne dothe holde us from shewing hym that favoure that for the dutye wee owe unto you, the sight of your lyverye alone might otherwyse easelye bryng us unto. At the last quarter Sessions holden in this place, accused to be, and by good testimonye proved to be a person moche bent unto quarrelling. And here also then accused, and by like testimonye well proved to have uttered verye sclaunderous woordes against Mr Hendeleye (whom all wee and besyde us a great nomber, for his great yeres and vertuous course of lyfe, doo highlye esteeme), hee was by recognisaunce bounde to his good behavoure.

Sythens whiche tyme hee ys here also shrewdelye suspected to have corrupted sondrye bagges of woade, the doying wherof dyd tende to the great losse and hynderaunce of dyvers honest personnes

The consideracõn of whiche thinges thus layed together hathe inforced us in this Sessions towarde hym to doo as moche as wee dyd in the last Sessions. Wherof (and so of the disposition of the persoun hym selfe), wee thought meete to advertise your good Lordeshippe. And thus wee beseeche the Lorde in honorable estate to sende you a course of many joyfull yeres.

From Maydeston the XXVth of September 1582 Humblie at the commandement of your good Lordeshippe.

It is perhaps unnecessary to say that this letter is addressed to Ambrose Dudley, created Earl of Warwick in 1561, and brother of the Earl of Leicester. This Lord Warwick died without issue in 1590.

The man Wandenne had been mentioned in the report to the Privy Council in 1576 (see No. IX). He was clearly a complete rogue.

The bags which he adulterated contained woad, *Isatis tinctoria*, from which the blue dye was obtained.[1]

XXXVII. *To the right worshipfull his very loving frende Edward Boys Esquire*

Great pitie were yt that outwarde sute for Landes or Goodes (and therby cause of inwarde unkyndenesse), sholde aryse betwene you and the right honorable the Lorde cheefe Baron. I maye (and emong other of your frendes I doo), rather greatlye bewayle yt, then fynde mee selfe hable in suche sorte as I wolde (that ys wythe the good contentation of bothe sydes), finallye to ende yt. Yf the Lorde suffer mee to go unto London, and that I be there requyred to heare that that everye of you, for everye of you hathe in this case to saye,—I wyll therin (God wylling), wythe an indifferent respecte tell you myne opinion, and leave you bothe as your selfes shall thincke best, to use yt or refuse yt. Good Sir, sende unto Mr Cartwright the Lrẽ herein inclosed and the iiij^h wch by this bearer I sende you. And thus wythe my right hartie coñendacõns for this tyme I take my leave of you. From my howse in Bocton Malherbe this Thursdaye the xviij^th of October 1582.

Your very loving frende

Fynding that yor messenger was in yeres a Boye, and for Countrye an Iryshe Boye, and that his contynuaunce wythe you had ben little more then one yere, I have here stayed the iiij^h, and meane as shortlye as I can to sende yt to my Brother Erasmus Fynche, to be by hym sent unto you, untill wch tyme, I praye you in your handes retayne the Letter directed to Mr Cartwright.

The addressee may have been Edward, son of William Boys, of Fredville, Bonnington. He was Sheriff in 1577, and died on 15 February 1599, aged seventy-one.[2]

He, like Lord Cobham, had lost trust in the Lord Chief Baron; see No. XLIII.

---

[1] This is mentioned because about this time a plant was being grown in Kent called weld or wold, *Reseda Luteola*. From this a yellow dye was made.

[2] Berry, *Genealogies of Kent*, p. 441. In the Ingoldsby Family Legend called *The Wedding Day* the bridegroom was 'Fredville's hope, young Valentine Boys'.

Erasmus Finch was the second son of Sir William Finch, by his second wife, Catherine Gainsford. He was Captain of Deal Castle,[1] and Captain of the Canterbury Trainband in 1588.[2] It was his sister Eleanor whose second husband was Thomas Wotton, which explains 'my Brother'. Another brother of Mrs. Wotton has been mentioned in the note to No. XXIX.

XXXVIII. *To his very loving frende M*^{r}* Thomas Cartwright*

That that I have seene to be very well written by you, and that that by others reaporte in other partes, I have hearde to be well done by you,—have made mee many tymes right sorie that (for a thing in substance of Christian religion amounting, as I thought, almost to nothing), this Realme being your naturall Countreye. In this Realme this Churche wherof you were by profession a right woorthye minister, that sondrie of your acquayntance being your good frendes, sholde lacke the comforte of your presence. But I doo nowe too too late speake of yt, when thinges passed mayebe rather repented then revoked. For your good Letter, full of good Councell, I doo right hartelye thancke you. Good Mr Cartwright, in your prayers commende thende of my lyfe (wch I hope ys at hande), to the mercye of Almightie God in Christe my savioure, I have sent Mr Boys for you, and intreated hym to sende unto you iiij^{li}, I praye you as a little token of my good wyll receyve yt, and as your awne use yt. And so wth my right hartie commendacõns for this tyme I take my leave of you.

From my howse in Bocton Malherbe this Thursdaye the xviijth of October 1582.

Your very loving frende

Thomas Cartwright matriculated at Clare Hall in 1541; he left during the reign of Queen Mary, but returned and went to Trinity College in 1560, and was made a Fellow in 1562. He was deprived in 1571 and went to Geneva, returning the next year. He was called the coryphaeus of early Nonconformity, with good reason. His learning was admitted,

[1] Bryan I'Anson, *History of the Finch Family*, 1933, p. 20.
[2] Muster documents of Canterbury, Nos. 1 and 2. For this note Dr. Urry, F.S.A., is sincerely thanked.

but he was a disappointed man, with a most unpleasant character.[1] The Earl of Leicester was his protector, and that may have influenced Wotton's opinion of him; after the Earl's death in 1589 he was brought before a Commission and committed to prison, from which he was released by the influence of Whitgift, his enemy in controversy.

It is interesting to see Wotton sends him £4, because Cartwright acquired wealth by land-jobbing after Wotton's death.[2]

Thomas Wotton's uncle, the Dean, thought less of Cartwright perhaps, for in 1564 he had asked to see the archives at Canterbury; the Dean wrote his permission on condition that he was not allowed in the Treasury, but that Mr. Butler should get out all the writings 'that shall serve' for his inspection.[3]

XXXIX. *To the right worshipfull his very loving sonne George Morton Esquire*

That that Mr Fuller dyd latelie sende unto mee herein inclosed I sende unto you.

As a wyse man I praye you to consider your expenses, as lyving upon your awne, ye maye wythe your awne leave unto your vertuous wyfe and sweete Babes a signification of the Dutye ye owe theym. As a good man so consider your promesses, as that maye be done dulye that ye have said sholde be done assuredlye. Sende unto mee the Bonde I praye you that made to Ambrose Smythe at your request I entered into.

And so wythe my right hartie commendacõns for this tyme, I take my leave of you.

From my howse in Bocton Malherbe this Mondaye the xxij^th of October 1582.

Your very loving father.

This letter was written three months after the former one to Morton; it is written in a charitable spirit, and concludes quite warmly.

The next letter bears no name and is written four months after No. XXXIX. It is a letter of condolence, and possibly it was sent to

---

[1] It is developed in some detail by Isaac D'Israeli in his article on Martin Marprelate, *Quarrels of Authors*.

[2] Fuller says that Cartwright was 'growing rich in Warwick by the bounty of his followers' in 1602 (*Church History*, bk. x, sect. i, § 7).

[3] C. E. Woodruffe and Wm. D'Auks, *Memorials of Canterbury*, 1912, p. 391.

Morton, as a hint to him to 'lyve vertuouslye' after he had sustained a loss by death.

No. XLI also bears no name, but is clearly to Morton. It was written within three months of No. XL, and closes the sad story of the stepson, as a note to No. XLI proves.

XL

They lyve (while they lyve), happelye that lyve vertuouslye, They dye blessedlye that in the Lorde dye faythfullye. They that thus doo feele the Comforte of their awne doyng And this waye reposed in the place of perpetuall felicitie, They have for theym selfes made a most blessed chaunge Wee that in the persounes of other see this to be done, the neerer in nature they be unto us, the greater cause of Joye doo they offer us. Lyfe and Deathe hang upon the wyll of the Lorde, Hee dothe nothing that ys yll done, or unmeete for theym to whom yt ys done[1] Hee that makethe other construction myssethe moche the matter. And I hope that the consideration of this poynt wyll (and I doo most earnestlye intreate you that the consideration of this poynt maye), moche diminishe the cause of your greefe. In this matter at this tyme more I cannot saie, and therfore here for this tyme shortlye I make an ende.

From my howse in Bocton Malherbe this Thursdaye the xxviij[th] of Februarie 1582

XLI. *(No name, but certainly to George Morton)*

Yf ye laye awaye that reverende regarde that in honest thinges ye doo by dutie owe unto mee, ye will (against my will) heavelye constrayne mee to laye awaye that love that in nature I owe unto you.

And smallye doe ye regarde or esteeme mee, when to my great greefe I maye playnelye see that ye spende so precious a thing as tyme ys idellye (whiche ys yll), or in lewde playe (wch ys woorse) and that playe manye tymes accompanyed wth wicked Othes

---

[1] Above the word 'done' is a caret and 'Of lyfe and deathe' written above; probably it belongs to the next sentence.

(wch ys woorst of all). From the eyes of mee alone, being but one, and often from you, ye maye sometyme holde theese thinges from the eyes of all men, and from the eyes of Almightie God (the maker and conserver of all men), ye can never hyde or holde anye (the leaste) of theese thinges.

I doo in this place, in this tyme hereupon streightlye charge you that I maye not hereafter wythe myne eyes see, or by true rea-porte heare, that ye doo wythe any of my servauntes playe at dyce, tables, or Cardes, or upon any occasion use any wicked Othe.

And yf yet against that that I have alredye often said, and doo nowe saie unto you, ye will still from your Booke spende your tyme Idellye, or wythe a sorte of rascall Boyes accompanye your selfe baselye, the greefe ys nowe myne,—the shame alredye ys, and the losse will hereafter be youres. From my howse in Saynte Marye Craye this Thursdaye the xvj^th of Maye 1583.

Your father.

This is the last letter to Morton; the threat in the closing words was carried out, as Thomas Wotton's will[1] proves:

Whereas during my life and the life of my said wyfe [Heleenor] by a composition in worde passed betweene myselfe of thone parte and George Morton Esq. her sonne of thother parte, I oughte owte of the mannor of Pytney Loitye, C° Somerset, yearly to have had the Some of £25, and after by a sufficient assurance in writing (which to my own use I have lefte in the handes of my said wiffe), the yearly some of £23, and whereas that after 6 years and a halfe ended at the Feast of St Michael Tharchangel last 1586, was due unto me a hundred three score two pounds ten shillings, the one halfe whereof I do entreate my wiffe to give to Mary Morton, nowe the wiffe of the said George Morton, to thende that the same may be of some com-forte to her.

George Morton may have been a ne'er-do-well, or merely tactless in dealing with a stepfather who was so rigid a moralist as to regard his 'woorst of all' offence swearing when he lost at dice or cards. An oath might well earn reprimand, but not complete disherison.

[1] P.C.C. 4 Spencer 1586/7.

XLII. *To the right worshipfull his verye loving frende John Tufton Esquire*

After my right hartie commendacõns, the state of Rochester Brydge, (by a course of long tyme and smale regarde of some inferioure officers, fallen into great decaye), dothe constrayne mee nowe by Letter (as I have alredye done by mouthe), to intreate you that some rounde portion of that that your late woorthye father hathe appoynted to be bestowed on highe wayes, maye be bestowed upon this waye. For common Roade none ys more usuall; in use, none more necessarie; in substance and fourme, none more notable.

We will, of your bountie upon this thing thus bestowed, make a good note, and leave unto you and your name emong suche as have of late tyme furthered the good estate of this Bridge, the first and cheef place. And for mee selfe in particuler I shall surelye accompt that ye doo this waye as moche pleasure mee, as thoughe ye dyd to myne awne use bestowe this good somme upon mee. Under wch termes I commende this thing unto you, and your selfe to the favour of Almightie God. From my howse in Cobham this Saturdaye the xxijth of June, 1583.

John Tufton, of Hothfield about half-way between Boughton Malherbe and Ashford, was son of another John, who died in 1567. He was Sheriff in 1576, and was made a baronet in 1611, dying in 1624.

A later Sir John married Margaret, daughter of the second Lord Wotton, and therefore great-granddaughter of our letter-writer.

The Earls of Thanet descended from the first Sir John.

This is one of several letters which Thomas Wotton wrote in his efforts to preserve Rochester Bridge; in No. XLVIII he asks Tufton for another donation. Thomas had been a commissioner for its repair in 1561,[1] and was now working hard to save it, making the handsome contribution of £78 himself, as No. LI shows.

Just over a hundred years after Thomas Wotton died, a lady rode over his bridge on her way to Dover; her account of it would have pleased him, so would her Nonconformity. Celia Fiennes wrote: 'The Bridg at Rochester is the finest in England—nay its said to Equal any in the world—it is not built upon wth houses as London Bridge but its very Long and fine, Iron spikes Like a grate is on the top of the wall

[1] *Archaeologia Cantiana*, vol. xvii, p. 238, in an article by A. A. Arnold.

w[ch] is breast high, and these irons on the top w[ch] are above a yard more. Its indented at Each arch as all bridges are, there are 9 large Arches wth y[e] middle one w[ch] is to be opened by drawing up to give passage to Barges and little vessells. When y[e] tide was out I saw the worke of the arches is wth wood Cutt hollow, and stands a good distance into the water to keep the water from bearing too hard against the Bridge.'[1]

XLIII. *To the right honorable S[r] Roger Manwoode, Knighte Lorde Cheefe Baron*

Not long after I had yesterdaye written and sealed the Letter w[ch] I dyd, then by the handes of a servaunt of my cousin Moyle Fynche sende unto your good Lordeshippe, hither came a servaunt of M[r] Doctor Lakes, wythe suche a Letter under your hande, and under the handes of M[r] Deane of Canterburye, M[r] Boys, and others,—as unto the right honorable the Busshoppe of Dover, Nicholas Sentleger, and mee selfe seemed surelye verye straunge.

Never was yt seene (I recken) that some Commissioners (in a Commission of so great majestie as the Commission for causes ecclesiasticall ys thought to be), sholde directlye inhibit that that ys orderlye appoynted to be done by some other Commissioners (where bothe thone and thother ar of equall aucthoritie). Your good Lordeshippe dothe right well knowe that this Commission tyethe none of the Commissioners to any place. And yf yt dyd respecte one place afore an other, this place, regarding the proximitie of places and the condition of some of the Commissioners was a verye meete place to have suche causes treated in, as M[r] Doctor Lakes sholde here have ben charged wythe, seyng that in the paryshe of Edgerton most of theym doo dwell that in the said causes have ought to saie, and seyng that that paryshe ys from hence little more then one myle, and seyng that of the Commissioners hee that from his howse had most to go, had scarce yet vij myle to go. Besyde this emong us was yt here also thought and said that that Letter imported thus moche, as that w[th]out the assistance of your good Lordeshippe and the rest

[1] Celia Fiennes, *Through England on a Side Saddle*, 1888, p. 100.

for lacke of aucthoritie wee might not heare, (or for lacke of indifferencie meete men wee were not to heare), that that Mr Doctor Lakes sholde here have ben charged wythe, The consideration and weight of the last of wch ij poyntes, (being of bothe the greater), was unto us all surelye a matter of moche greefe. The acquayntaunce and familiaritie that have a long tyme ben betweene your good Lordeshippe and mee; During that tyme the great comforte that I have had by your good countenaunce and Councell doo constrayne mee in a frendelye sorte to write thus moche unto you, some parte wherof I have also written to Mr Deane and Mr Boys. And so doo I meane for my parte here to have yt ende. From my howse in Bocton Malherbe this Tuysdaye the seconde of Julye 1583. Your assured loving cousin and frende.

Sir Roger Manwood was born in 1525, the son of a draper at Sandwich. He was called to the Bar in 1555, and made Recorder of Sandwich; he was also M.P. for Hastings. In 1571 he was made a Justice of Common Pleas, and Chief Baron of the Exchequer on 17 November 1578, and knighted.

His character was of singular complexity. He was active in promoting useful works; for instance he had helped to save Wotton's pet, Rochester Bridge, and to regulate the lands with which it was endowed. He built seven almshouses at Hackington, and aided other good works.

Yet he was 'ambitious and arbitrary, and somewhat regardless of the means by which he obtained the objects on which he had set his heart'.[1] The school which he founded at Sandwich, at first with the support of Archbishop Parker, has been mentioned in the note to No. I. The way in which he 'endowed' it (retaining the rents for himself whilst he lived, and paying the master's stipend) inevitably led to litigation in his grandson's day.[2]

After Wotton's death he was found in 1591 to have sold an office which was in his gift, and various perversions of justice were alleged against him. The present letter names Nicholas St. Leger as Suffragan Bishop of Dover, but it was Richard Rogers, another Suffragan of Dover, who brought up a case against him of having sold the Queen's pardon in a case of murder for £240. There had been a bad murder in Canterbury, and Manwood undertook to bring the assailant to justice. Actually he was pardoned, and appeared clad in Manwood's livery. His

---

[1] Partly from the *D.N.B.*, but more from Foss's *Dictionary of Judges*, 1870, p. 430.

[2] W. Boys, *History of Sandwich*, 1792, where there is a pedigree, plate of his monument, and facsimile of his writing.

father was a rich brewer. The many complaints against Manwood led him to seek Burleigh's protection—he did not obtain it.

With all his failings he was 'pious and charitable, and a kind-hearted man'. He took care to have the very ostentatious monument in Sandwich Church erected whilst he was alive.[1]

Moyle Finch was son of Sir Thomas Finch, of Eastwell, by his wife Catherine Moyle. He was M.P. for the County 1593, baronet 1611, and died in 1614.[1]

Dr. Stephen Lakes was the official of the Archdeacon of Canterbury, and presided over the archidiaconal courts, signing the depositions in the margin.[2] He lived latterly at St. Stephen's, selling his house in 1604.

The Dean at this date was the Richard Rogers who has been mentioned above.[3]

Egerton is about equidistant from Boughton Malherbe on the south-east, and from Charing on the south-west.

XLIV. *To the right worshipfull his verye assured loving frende Sᵣ Thomas Sondes, knight*

The bounteous course ye keepe in your howse, your good disposition towarde all good thinges out of your howse, doo incourage mee, and the necessitie of Rochester Brydge (wherof I am an unworthie Officer), dothe constrayne mee to crave that of you that you ar willing to geve. Beggers you knowe ar not allowed to be choosers, and therfore this request maye not go further then shall stande wythe your good pleasure. The waye for trade ys usuall, in use very necessarie, in substance and shewe verye notable, in woorke verye chargeable, and in this tyme so moche decayed, as the Revenue apperteynyng unto yt ys no wayes hable to upholde yt. Yf you shall not like this Letter, thincke, good sir, that yt was then never written unto you. And thus right gladde to heare of your good estate, whiche I beseeche the Lorde long to contynue, for this tyme I take my leave of you. From my howse in Bocton Malherbe this Weddensdaye the thirde of Julye 1583.

Sir Thomas was the son of Anthony Sandes, of Throwley (where there

---

[1] *Archaeologia Cantiana*, vol. lviii, p. 19.
[2] From information most kindly given by Dr. Wm. Urry, F.S.A.
[3] Hasted, vol. i, p. 597.

are some good monuments to the family in the church). His first wife was the daughter of John Tufton; he had no children by her. He next married the daughter of William, tenth Lord Cobham. By her he was grandfather of the Earl of Feversham, with the subsidiary titles of Baron Throwley and Viscount Sandes.

XLV. *To the right honorable his very good Lorde the L. Cobham L. Warden of the fyve portes*

Comforte your selfe wythe the rememberaunce of the blessed chaunge your sonne my Cousyn hathe made, that losing earthe hathe gotten heaven, that for a short mortall lyfe (the course wherof might happelye have ben subjecte to sondrie sortes of sorrowes), lyvethe everlastinglye, and wythe the almightie and immortall God most joyfullye.

Comforte your selfe as a wyse man wythe the state of the thing that ys nowe brought to a poynt remedilesse. Comforte your selfe as a Christian man wythe the provydence and pleasure of almightie God whose power orderethe all thing, whose wysdome knowethe all thing, whose goodnesse procurethe no yll thing.

Comforte your selfe for your good Ladye, and other the cheefe of your familie, that by your example maye wth some good patience receyve God's gratious visitation.

Comforte your selfe for your frendes and Countrye that have good interest in you, and wth good myndes wyshe well unto you. Comforte your selfe for your selfe, that lyving here (as ye maye), in mynde joyfullye, ye maye (yf the Lorde so wyll), long lyve here in Bodye helthelye. Hearing of the deathe of your said sonne yesterdaye, I have written this thing unto your good Lordeshippe this daye, sondrie of your good frendes can doo yt more largelye and wyselye (none can doo yt more faythfullye), then I have done. And so I beseeche the Lorde in honorable estate to sende you a course of many joyfull yeres.

From my howse in Bocton Malherbe this frydaye the ix^th of August 1583.

Your most bounden

This is the letter of condolence upon the death of Maximilian Brooke, to whom No. XV was addressed in 1577.

It is curious, but the *Complete Peerage*, 1913, gives the date of Maximilian's death as 5 December 1583, and his age as twenty-three.[1] He had been born on 4 December 1560, as noted under No. XV, and the present letter proves that he died before 8 August, and was twenty-two.

XLVI. *To the right worshipfull his very assured loving Cousyn Sʳ Edwarde Hoby, knight*

So manye personnes of so great worshippe and wysdome ar so well chosen to heare and order the man and matter mentioned in the Letters of the right worshipfull the Justicers of Assise as for nomber wee neede not, and for good discretion better cannot, be therunto appoynted; among wᶜʰ wᵗʰout aucthoritie I meane not to intrude mee selfe. I doo neverthelesse towarde this man in this matter intreate you to be as good as by the rules of justice and equitie ye maye convenientlye be. And thus, my good knight, for this tyme in hast I take my leave of you.

From my howse in Bocton Malherbe this Mondaye the 12 of August 1583.

Your assured loving Cousyn

Sir Edward Hoby was born at Bisham, Berks., about 1560. He was made Constable of Queenborough Castle in 1582. He was a man of considerable ability, and wrote some polemical pamphlets, one called *A Counter-snarl for Ishmael Rabshakah*, 1613, and when a Jesuit answered it, countered with *A Currycombe for a Coxcombe*, 1615.[2]

He was M.P. for Kent in 1593, in which year the Queen granted him a life-lease of Shurland. He died at Queenborough Castle in 1617, and was buried in the Hoby Chapel at Bisham. His mother was Elizabeth, daughter of Sir Anthony Cooke (see No. I).

XLVII. *To the right worshipfull his very loving Cousyn Thomas Smythe Esquire*

Towarde the contynuance of a thing in matter so notable, in trade so usuall, in use so necessarie, in tyme so auncient, and by

---

[1] This is also in the first G.E.C. edition of 1889.
[2] Wood's *Athenae Oxonienses*, vol. ii, col. 195.

tyme and some negligence in some former inferioure officers, so ruinous as ys the Brydge of Rochester, no other thing ys ment to move you then your awne good disposition towarde good purposes well bent of thone syde, and the blessinges of almightie God in abundaunt measure mercifullye bestowed upon you of thother syde. That that towarde this good thing ye have ment to doo, doo yt, my good Cousyn, somewhat the rather for my sake willinglye, and as your good mynde and estate shall serve you, bountifullye. I have of very purpose sent this bearer my servaunt to you for yt, the doyng wherof I praye you take in good parte. And thus wythe my right hartie commendacõns for this tyme I take my leave of you.

From my howse in Bocton Malherbe this Saturdaye the xvij[th] of August 1583.

Your very loving Cousyn

This letter is to Thomas Smith, commonly called The Customer, because he farmed the customs of the Port of London. In 1585 he was granted the manor of Westenhanger, or Ostenhanger, in the parish of Stanford, north-west of Hythe. In his day the Castle retained its fifteenth-century importance. He died on 7 June 1591, and was succeeded by his son John, who was Sheriff in 1600 and was father of Thomas, created Viscount Strangford.[1] Another son of Customer Smith was Richard, who acquired Leeds Castle by exchange and married Elizabeth, daughter of Sir Thomas Scott, of Scott's Hall.[2]

XLVIII. *To the right worshipfull his very loving frende John Tufton Esquire*

Of the somme by your late father (of vertuous memorie), geven towarde thamendement of highe wayes, you can upon no waye bestowe any portion that better deservethe the name of a highe waye then this, you can upon no waye bestowe any portion where yourselfe and your frendes shall receyve the comforte of your charge more then upon this. Yf yt maye like you of your goodnesse to geve us one Twentie marke more, wee wyll therin never

---

[1] Hasted, vol. iii, p. 325; *Arch. Cant.*, vol. xx, p. 76, for pedigree.

[2] Berry's *Genealogies*, p. 250.

trouble you more. Towarde whiche, good Sir, let my intreatie so farre furthe move you as in reason yt maye move you.

And thus commending this matter unto you, and your selfe to the favo^r of Almightie God, for this tyme I take my leave of you. From my howse in Bocton Malherbe this Saturdaye the xvijth of August 1583.

Your very loving frende

[The effecte of the first parte of this Letter ys conteyned in the first parte of the Lrẽ above directed to Mr Smythe.]

XLIX. [*No name*]

Little needethe hee, whose cause ys brought afore you, in the favoure of hym self; to present eyther his awne petition or the Letters of any other, unto you.

And yet the requestes of sondrie my good frendes and neighboures thinhabitauntes of the hundred of Rakesleye (wherof upon good respectes I must accompt mee selfe a dutifull member), have drawen mee to that that towarde you for your selfes ys needelesse, and towarde us the parties ys bootelesse, that ys, that towarde us the said inhabitauntes in the matter of Austen's Attaynt, ye will at my sute carye that favoure that ye maye fytlye shewe us, and that by your good mediation, wthout more adoo, the matter maye receyve a finall conclusion. Towarde whiche I am sure, without my Letters, ye will alone doo whatsoever ye maye doo.

And this wythe my right hartie commendacõns for this tyme, I take my leave of you.

From my howse in Bocton Malherbe this Weddensdaye the xvjth of October 1583.

Your assured loving frende.

Wotton calls himself 'a dutifull member' of the Hundred of Rakesley on account of his property in St. Mary Cray. The lathe of Sutton at Hone was divided into an Upper and Lower Division, and the Crays fell within the Hundred of Ruxley,[1] in the Upper Division.

The letter was obviously sent to his brother Justices.

The Austen on whose behalf this letter was sent has not been traced.

[1] So Kilburne spelt it in 1659, *A Survey*, p. 306.

Possibly he was connected with Robert Austen who purchased Hall Place, Bexley, in 1562,[1] that lay in the Hundred of Rakesley. His father was William Austen, of Heronden, Tenterden, which is in the lathe of Scray.

L. *To the right worshipfull his very loving frende Reginalde Scot Esquire*

So slowlye seemethe the pardon of Posyer to go further as afore the next assises, I doo therof conceyve little hope. And w^{th}out that pardon in suche estate standethe hee, as further then the next assises, of the lengthe of his lyfe by the tolleration of his Judges, I conceyve lesse hope. Towarde yt (considered bothe by the weake Bodye I have, and by the smale credit I have), so little can I doo, as whatsoever yt seemethe to be, nothing at all wyll yt in Deede be found to be. I doo not hereof thus wryte unto you, for that towarde the helpe of this poore prisoner any faulte ys to be founde in you; but that ye sholde wythe mee and others somewhat bewayle his condition, that after a course of moche myserie rysing by the nature of the place where hee ys (in hope of lyfe somewhat the better borne; that hope nowe gone), hee must in publique sorte shamefullye, wythe a heavie mynde, dolorouslye drawe his dayes to an ende. And so dothe that matter drawe this Letter to an ende.

From my howse in Bocton Malherbe this Frydaye the xxv^{th} of October 1583.

Your very loving frend

Reginald Scot was son of Richard, and nephew of Sir Reginald Scott, of Scott's Hall, Smeeth. He was born in 1541 and died in 1599.[2] He was therefore of kin to Sir Thomas Scott of No. LV. He is well known as the author of *The Discoverie of Witchcraft*, 1584, in which the two opening chapters of Book VII are filled with the story of Mildred, the base daughter of Alice Norrington, of Westwell, which is between Charing and Ashford. She saw visions and heard sounds, and perhaps was what

---

[1] Hasted, i. 160.

[2] J. R. Scott, *Scott of Scott's Hall*, 1876, p. 188. He is usually called Rainold, and when he married in 1568 it was as Reignold. He used only one 't' in his name on his title-page.

is now called a poltergeist. Reginald calls it 'ventriloquie and cousen-age', and her mother aided 'this bastardlie queane's enterprise'. He tells us that 'she was convented before M. Thomas Wotton, of Bocton Malherbe, a man of great worship and wisedome, and for deciding and ordering of matters in this commonwealth of rare and singular dexteritie'. He is too wordy to quote at length, and it must be reduced to saying that she 'shewed hir feats, illusions, and transes' in the presence of 'divers gentlemen and gentlewomen of great worship . . . at the house of the aforesaid Mr Wotton'. Thomas's 'discreet handling of the matter' exposed the fraud, 'and she received condigne punishment'. He does not make it clear what was her offence. She was only seventeen.

Rainold Scot also wrote *A Perfect Platform of a Hop-Garden*, 1576.

LI. *To the right honorable his verye good Ladye the Countesse of Pembrooke*

You maye saie, Good madame, that I doo in a presumptuous sorte moche forget mee selfe in the first Letter that ever I sent you, and afore that ever I spake wythe you, in a matter of charge to present a petition unto you.

The reaporte of your great curtesye and bountie of thone syde dothe incourage mee; the necessitie of the thing I have in hande of thother syde dothe constrayne mee unto yt. Yf emong other of your most vertuous actions, yt might please you to bestowe some good portion of moneye upon Rochester Brydge, you shall hardelye bestowe yt upon any persounes that wyll more grate-fullye receyve yt then th officers of that Brydge, (wherof un-woorthelye I am one), you can hardlye bestowe yt upon any woorke that ys in shewe more bewtifull; in stuffe or matter more notable; in trade more usuall; in use more necessarye; and in present estate more ruinous then Rochester Brydge. Yf I had not this Sommer of myne awne moneye bestowed upon yt lxxviijˡⁱ yt had surelye fallen into a verye great decaye.

You knowe, right vertuous Ladye, that Beggars maye be no choosers; towarde this good purpose appoynt what ye will, and when ye will. I will therof, God willing, towarde a continuall rememberance of your most vertuous disposition emong our recordes make a speciall note.

And thus I beseeche the Almightie God in honorable estate to sende you a course of many joyfull yeres.

From my howse in Saynte Marye Craye the vj[th] of December 1583

Humblie at the comaundement of your good Ladyshippe.

Although it was seen (Letter V) that Wotton was a friend of Sir Henry Sidney, it appears, from the opening of this letter, that he had little personal acquaintance with this daughter of Sir Henry's, who was destined to become famous after Wotton's death. In 1577 she became the third wife of Henry, second Earl of Pembroke; her uncle the Earl of Leicester arranged the marriage and found part of her dowry.[1] In 1590 her brother, Sir Philip Sidney, published *The Countess of Pembroke's Arcadia*. She was then mother of William, who became the third Earl of Pembroke and is best known to us as the subject of one of Lord Clarendon's brilliant characters.[2] Thus was justified William Browne's Epitaph, with the line: 'Sidney's sister, Pembroke's mother.'

LII. *To the right honorable his verye good Lorde the Lorde Burghleye, Lorde Treasurer of Englande*

Yf the rest of suche Bookes or notes remaynyng yet in my handes as in any of my late uncle's late legations, passed under his penne, maye in any wyse stande your good Lordeshippe in any stedde, I doo by this bearer my servaunt sende theym wholye unto you. For the present applyeng of one parte of theym yf you maye fynde that parte emong theym, wee maye justlye saie that happie ys her Ma[tie] that hathe suche a Councelloure, happie ys the Realme that hathe suche a member as unto the one and in the other you are well knowne to be.

In whiche course under her said Ma[tie] I beseeche the Almightie God to sende you a course of many joyfull yeres.

From Pykering howse in London the   of Januarye 1583.

The original of this letter is in the British Museum, and is reproduced at page 60, whilst the copy in the letter-book is shown at page 61.

[1] Sir Henry's acknowledgement is in a letter from him to the Earl, A. Collins's *Sidney Papers*, p. 97.

[2] It is lengthy, but fair, and his many unselfish qualities are balanced by 'some allay of vice'.

Letter actually sent to Lord Burleigh

It is printed by the courtesy of the Keeper of MSS., British Museum

Letter to Lord Burleigh in the letter-book

The letter, with the Dean's papers, was sent to Burleigh's house in the Strand. Exeter Street and Burleigh Street mark the site. A member of Burleigh's staff docketed the letter 'Mr Thomas Wootton. Certaine Notes of D. Wootton's Legations', which shows that he looked very carelessly at the bold signature before his eyes.

Nicholas Wotton was an outstanding character at any date. He was born in 1496, and was presented by his father in 1517 to the living of Boughton Malherbe, of which Sir Robert was patron. Tunstall, Bishop of London, made Dr. Nicholas his Official in 1528. In 1540 he was made Archdeacon of Worcester, and in 1541 he became the first Protestant Dean of Canterbury. In 1544 he was made Dean of York, and retained both deaneries until his death.[1] Neither diocese can have seen much of him, for he was excellent as a diplomat, and much of his time must have been spent abroad. Walton says that he served on nine embassies to foreign princes.

A single legation may be mentioned, because he was joined with Lord Burleigh in making the Treaty of Leith in 1560, after the French partisans of Mary Queen of Scots found they could no longer hold that town against the English, who had been called in by the Scots. We are told that Queen Elizabeth sent: 'William Cecill, Knight, her principal Secretary, and with him Doctor Wotton, Deane of Canterbury and of Yorke, and one of the privie councell, furnished with ample authoritie to deale in these affaires.'[2]

No ordinary man could have served in succession and satisfied Henry VIII, Edward VI, Mary, and Elizabeth. Perhaps it is most neatly put by Fuller: 'He was a doctor of both laws, and some will say of both Gospels, . . . he never overstrained his conscience, such his oily compliance in all alterations.'[3]

He was one of those who dined in 'Sir William Cicell's chamber' at Windsor on 10 December 1563. Ascham says that Dean Wotton, 'a man milde of nature, with soft voice and fewe wordes', agreed with his host's views as to gentle methods in education.[4] With this view the Dean's nephew would certainly have concurred, for we saw him in Letter No. I ask for a master 'farre from rage or furie'.

The Dean made Thomas heir of what little estate he had, and Thomas put up a fine monument to his uncle in Trinity Chapel, Canterbury

[1] According to Woodruff, *Memorials of Canterbury*, p. 395, Dr. Wotton was allowed to keep the two Deaneries as an easy way of remunerating him for his diplomatic services.

[2] Sir John Hayward, *Annals of Queen Elizabeth*, 1840, p. 68. Stow adds the name of Sir William Cordall to the other two.

[3] *Church History*, bk. ix, sect. ii, § 11.

[4] Preface to the *Scholemaster*, 1570.

Cathedral, with an immensely long inscription in Latin, which ends with an excellent personal description: 'Corpus illi erat gracile quidem, et parvum sed erectum, habitudo sana, vultus liberalis.'[1] The kneeling figure was carved in Italy, where the sculptor had modelled his head when the Dean was at Rome. He died in London on 26 January 1567.

LIII. *To the right honorable Sir Frauncis Walsingham knight, her Maties Principall Secretarye*

Aged as I am, and about myne age weake as I am, and therby like shortlye to leave a woorke unto others as executoures unto mee selfe, I can hardelye take in hande a woorke as an executoure unto an other. Th execution of the Testament of Sir Thomas Walsingham by mee upon this reason renunced. I doo most humblie beseeche you, good Sir, to receyve in good parte.

And thus I beseeche the Almightie God in honorable estate to sende you a course of many joyfull yeres.

From Pykering howse in London the   of Januarye 1583

Sir Thomas Walsingham, of Scadbury, Chislehurst, was a cousin of Sir Francis, who had sold his property at Foots Cray in 1578 and thereafter had none himself in Kent. Sir Thomas was a patron of Marlowe, who was a visitor at Scadbury, certainly in 1593.[2] When Sir Francis died in 1590, Thomas Watson wrote an eclogue called *Melibœus* in Latin and English. It was dedicated to Sir Thomas, who is represented by the character of Tityrus; Sir Francis was Melibœus.

Thomas Wotton was well advised to decline to be executor, for he died just five years after this letter was written, when he was sixty-six, Letter No. XXIX shows that he called himself 'an olde man' when he was fifty-nine. Walton says that both Thomas and his uncle the Dean foresaw the very days on which they would die, explaining it rather inconsequently by saying that both were 'men of holy lives, of even tempers, and much given to fasting and prayer'.

[1] J. Meadows Cowper, *Memorial Inscriptions . . . Canterbury*, 1897, p. 133.
[2] *Archaeologia Cantiana*, vol. lxix. 219.

LIV. *To the right honorable their verye good Lordes the Lordes of her Maties most honorable Preevye Councell*

Howe redelye your good Lordeshippes have ben alwayes bent towarde the reliefe of suche as be or in good causes ar like to be oppressed, ys to your great commendation and the comforte of those that by petition have presented theym selfes unto you, right well knowne to the worlde.

So yt ys, right honorable, that sondrie ministers and preachers of the woorde of God within the countie of Kent have ben latelye by the Archebusshoppe of Canterburye suspended, and as wee feare upon that suspention ar like from their ecclesiasticall functions to be wholye removed, as by their awne Supplication, in humble sorte presented unto your good Lordeshippes, ys made knowne unto you, and by their reaporte made knowne unto us. None can better tell then wee that theese men, or the most parte of theese men, resiaunt still in their awne charges, doo unto their awne parisshioners preache very christianlye, and emong theym lyve right vertuouslye. None can better tell then wee, that a great nomber of thinhabitauntes of this Countie by this good preaching accompanyed wythe a course of vertuous lyving, have ben brought w^{th}out sute emong theym selfes to lyve quyetlye; and, in thexecution of your or her Maties commaundementes, verye obedientlye. None can better tell then wee that this great nomber of good persounes ar by this suspention or deprivation like a long tyme to lose that christian comforte that, thoroughe the preaching of theese good Ministers, they have made and still doo make a great accompt of. And howesoever yt ys that for conscience sake they seeme that they cannot by Othes in everye poynt approve the Booke that they sholde thus allow of. Yet none can better tell then wee that against this Booke none of theym (or verye fewe of theym), have ever preached, or ever ment to preache.

And (yf under the favoure of your good Lordeshippes without offence of the said Archebusshoppe wee maye saie yt), wee thincke that the measure ys somewhat harde, that a sorte of so well learned and vertuous Ministers sholde in lacke of the allowance of suche a Booke be suspended or deprived, as against wch booke (in their service duylye using yt, and in most poyntes for their myndes right well allowing yt), they never preached or ever ment to preache. This thing, and in this thing the course of theese good Ministers in fewe woordes thus layed open unto your good Lordeshippes, wee doo for theym (and in theym for our selfes), most humblie beseeche you (yf yt maye so stande wythe your good pleasures), so to deale wythe the said Archebusshoppe as they maye agayne be restored unto, and suffered to contynue in their said ecclesiasticall functions, untill they shall upon some other cause justlye deserve that, that upon this meane cause ys, (as wee thincke), verye heavelye layed upon theym. They shall be bounde perpetuallye to praye for you; wee shall for theym (and in theym for our selfes), be bounde still to honoure you. The Lorde shall of his mercye for yt hereafter in heaven re-warde you.

This letter was written in 1583, in support of a petition to the Privy Council from Kentish incumbents who had not complied with the clause in the Act of 1571, which required an incumbent, within two months of his induction, to read the Thirty-nine Articles in his church 'in the time of common prayer with a declaration of his unfaigned assent thereto'.[1] Whitgift had just been appointed Archbishop and was determined to enforce the law, which had been ignored for eleven years. The petition of the Kentish ministers is given by Fuller; it was sent, together with a similar one from Suffolk ministers, by the Privy Council to Whitgift. In his reply the Archbishop says that most of the Kentish petitioners were 'unlearned and young, such as I would be loathe to admit into the ministry, much less to allow as preachers'. They had visited him in a body and he had been obliged to listen to them for two days. This explains the little touch of acerbity which makes him wonder how they 'dare presume to bring my doings against them into question before your lordships'. He concluded that 'they rather sought quarrel against the book than to be satisfied'.[2]

It will be seen from the final paragraph of our next letter, No. LV,

[1] Act 13 Eliz. Cap. XII To reforme certaine disorders touching Ministers of the Church.

[2] *Church History*, bk. ix, sect. v, §§ 10, 11, and 22. If the names of the Kentish petitioners had been recorded, it would have been easy to see whether they were restored to their livings. Two of the documents printed by Fuller are in Lambeth Palace Library, MS. 577 (ff. 237–48). Mrs. Owen, deputy archivist, is thanked for this information.

that Wotton had been to see the Archbishop and had admitted that 'one or two' had put themselves in the wrong, but that should not 'tende to the obloquie of theym all'.

Eventually Whitgift yielded a little, because in 1583 he wrote to Sir Francis Walsingham, 'I have forborne to suspend or deprive any man already placed in any cure for not subscribing only, if hereafter he would promise unto me in writing the observing of the Book of Common Prayer, and the order of the Church by law laid down, and I do now require subscription to the said Articles of such only as are to be admitted to the ministry, and to ecclesiastical livings.'

LV. [*No name*]

Against sondrie so honest men, in a cause as I thincke generallye so good, commended by the petitions of so many by countrye and kynredde so neere you, and therby so well knowne unto you, without good cause by Letter secreatlye to oppose your selfe, was after yt was knowne (emong many other), verie greevous unto mee; as well bycause I had untill that tyme wythe mee selfe conceaved, and unto dyvers other spoken well of you, as also bycause that Letter caryde some suche matter as brought to a proofe, wyll I recken be founde untrue; the doyng wherof in thinges of so great weight ought to be farre from every honest man; farther from everye gentleman, and farthest from everye good christian man. This Letter strangelye brought to light made you emong many moche spoken of, and one tyme was yt said, (I assure you I knowe not nowe by whom), that you had towarde Sir Thomas Scot done some verie yll offices, as namelye in seeking to alienat from his eldest sonne his fatherlye affection, of whom upon verie good respectes sondrie suche as neerely knowe hym conceyved a verie good opinion. Hereupon yt might well be that I might saie I thought you had of his seconde sonne conceyved a verie good opinion, but that you had of his eldest sonne conceyved (and uttered unto mee) any yll opinion, I never said yt unto anye, and therfore none can trulye saie that ever I sholde so saie. You doo best knowe whether in abasing the Credit of that yong gentleman, ye have ought done, ye or no. Yf ye have nothing maye lightlie ether more or more often greeve you, then the certayne

knowledge of your awne unkynde demeanure. Yf the Letter said
to be your awne were never written by you, or being first upon
some heate happelye done, and after mysliked, were never sent
wythe your consent to th archebusshoppe, nor to none other that
might acquaynt hym wythe yt, moche wrong have you that ar
said to be in writing the authoure of yt, and in purpose the sender
of yt. That thing ys best knowne unto your selfe, And so unto
your selfe I leave yt. Towching the Ministers, a harde thing
surelye ys yt, that a fault or ii founde in one or two, sholde tende
to the obloquie of theym all, and that ys the course that bringethe
your Letter to that great lengthe that yt ys come unto; fewe of
those that in the behalfe of good Ministers have made their
humble sute unto th archebusshoppe, ment ever to speake for
suche as ar yll. And so was yt, in the first tyme that for this purpose wee were wythe hym, by mee selfe said unto hym. For your
Booke I doo right hartelye thancke you.
And thus I wyshe you alwayes right hartelye well to doo.

From my howse in Bocton Malherbe the xviiij[th] of Julye 1584.
Your loving frende.

Sir Thomas Scott, of Scott's Hall, Smeeth, was M.P. for the county in
1573 and 1588, and Sheriff in 1577, dying in 1594. By his first wife he
had a large family, and his eldest son Thomas succeeded him at Scott's
Hall, so that the ill-natured attempt to 'alienat from his eldest sonne his
fatherlye affection' properly failed.[1]

In the Armada year Sir Thomas was made commander of the Kentish
defence forces. His military exploits had to be *sine gloria*, but he was
made hero of a very dull ballad, first printed by Peck in 1740.[2]

LVI. *To the right honorable his verie good Lorde the L. Burghley L. Treasurer of Englande*

My bounden Duty unto your good Lordeshippe most humblie
remembered. This gentleman M[r] Brockehill (unto whom I am
for my dwelling a neere neighboure, and for my mynde a true

---

[1] Hasted, vol. iii, p. 292, and J. R. Scott, *Scott of Scott's Hall*, 1876, p. 254.
[2] *Historical Pieces*, vol. i, p. 29. It was later reprinted in full in *The World*, no. 133,
dated 17 July 1755, by Moore the editor.

frende), ys hee that by your Letters of an olde Date latelye delyvered unto hym, ys this yere appoynted to execute th office of the Escheatoure in the Countie of Kent. Hee and dyvers others ar wythe this office upon this respecte the more lothe to deale, that eyther the lacke of an Accompt, or an imperfect accompt of hym that in like office went next afore theym, sholde holde backe the passing of their Accomptes, howe perfecte and redye soever they sholde be founde to be. The inconvenience wherof in his fyt tyme can at the handes of none other receyve a more fyt and redye remedie, then at the handes of your good Lordeshippe, whose aucthoritie ys woorthelye verye great, whose wysdome ys playnlye seene to be greater, whose good mynde towarde good thinges ys greatest of all. I maye not in a matter so meane as this ys, in a tyme so full of busynesse of great moment as unto per- sounes so meane as I am, this ys thought to be, holde you wythe many woordes. And so I beseeche the almightie God in most honorable estate to sende you a course of many joyfull yeres.

From Pykering howse in London the xxvth of Januarie 1584.

Humblie at the commaundement of your good Lordeshippe.

'Mr Brockehill' may be Henry, son of Edward Brockhill of Aldington, Cobham. Henry died on 30 August 1596, aged sixty-three.[1]

The escheator was concerned with estates which, by the death of the owner intestate, might lapse to the Crown, or to the lord of the manor. The escheator for each county was appointed by the Lord Treasurer, and held office for one year.[2]

LVII

William Parry
was ap Harry
   by his name,
from the Alehowse
to the Galhowse
   grewe his fame.

Gotten westwarde
on a Bastarde
   was he thought,
Wherby one waye
kynne to Conwaye
   hathe hee sought.

[1] Hasted, vol. ii, p. 497.
[2] Jacob's *Law Dictionary*.

Like a Beast
wythe incest
 hee begonne,
Mother maryed
Daughter caryed
 hym a sonne.

Moche hee borrowed
Whiche hee sorrowed
 to repaye
Hare his Good
bought wythe blood,
 as they saye,

Yet for payment
had arraynment
 of his detter,
Shee that gave hym
lyfe to save hym,
 hang'd a better.

Parry his pardon
thought no guerdon
 for his woorthe,
Therfore sought
that hee mought
 travaile foorthe.

Whiche obtayned
hee remayned
 as before,

And wythe rashenes
shewed his basenes
 more and more.

Hee dyd enter
to adventer
 even her deathe,
by whose faver
hee dyd ever
 drawe his breathe.

Yt was pittie
One so wittie
 mal content,
Leaving reason
shoulde to treason
 so be bent.

But his gyftes
were but shyftes
 voyde of grace,
And his bravery
was but knavery
 bolde and base.

Wales dyd beare hym
Fraunce dyd sweare hym
 to the Pope,
Venice wrought hym
London brought hym
 to the Rope.

These verses have not been found in *Ballads . . . of the Elizabethan Period,*
printed by the Roxburghe Club, 1912, nor in other collections. In the
letter-book they follow a letter of 25 January 1584 and Parry was
executed on 2 March 1584, so they are clearly contemporary with that
event. Consummate villain as he was, Parry seems to have been acting
alone, though Walsingham sought some time for his accomplices,
which made Naunton 'seeke wherefore he suffered Parry to play so long
as he did on the hooke before he hoysed him up'.[1]

[1] In the life of Walsingham, included in *Fragmenta Regalia.*

There is a life of Parry added to *Megalopsychy*, 1682,[1] and it serves to explain a few points in our ballad.

Actually Parry was son of Harry ap David, who kept an alehouse at Northop, Co. Flint. His mother was daughter of a woman named Parry and a priest named Conway, whose parish was Halkin, which is about the same distance west of the town of Flint as Northop is south of it. Parry went to Chester as clerk to John Fisher, who had some knowledge of law. There he remained for some years, though often running away, so that his master shut him in 'a close place, chained, locked, and clogged'. He then ran away to London, and at this time changed his name to Parry and claimed kindred with the powerful Conway family of Portrethan, Flint. This explains the first two verses. He married two widows in succession. The first had 'some portion of wealth', which he quickly spent. The second was widow of Richard Heywood, and was old enough to be his mother, but had considerable wealth, which Parry soon dissipated. The dark story in the third verse may refer to her daughter. He then 'bought or begged the title of Doctor of Law'. Becoming indebted to Hugh Hare, of the Inner Temple, he attempted to murder him,[2] and was sentenced to death, but received the Queen's pardon. This explains the fourth stanza and the eighth, for he then went abroad, and the Jesuits made him undertake the murder of the Queen.[3]

The mention of France in the last verse seems to correspond with the statement, that, when he took oath at the altar, his 'two Beaupeers were the Cardinal of Vendôme and the Cardinal of Narbonne'.

When Parry received pardon for his assault on Hugh Hare and went abroad, apparently Lord Burleigh intended to use him as a spy, and he wrote to Anthony Bacon, then in Paris, to receive Parry. In consequence of this Anthony 'cultivated an intimate acquaintance with that dangerous traitor'. Leicester heard of this, and complained to the Queen about it, but 'the Lord Treasurer satisfied Her Majesty, engaging that his

---

[1] The main book is an account of the last seventeen years of the Queen's reign, by Sir William Monson and Heywood Townsend.

[2] Parry was himself of the Inner Temple; he went violently into the chamber of Hugh Hare, a barrister, 'and there grievously wounded him with a dagger, to the great peril of death'. It was ordered that 'Mr Parrie shall be henceforth no longer of this fellowship, but utterly expulsed for ever'. F. A. Inderwick, *Calendar of Inner Temple Records*, 1896, vol. i, p. 308.

[3] In the second part of *Robert Earl of Essex's Ghost*, which can be found in the *Harleian Miscellany*, it is said that Parry was 'instigated by Benedicto Palmio, and Cristofero de Salazar, secretary to Philip, to murder her Majesty, and Hannibal Cordreto, a Spanish priest, approved, etc.'. There is a metrical 'Epitaph' on Parry in the Calthorpe, or Elvetham, MSS. in the British Museum (vol. 31, fol. 191ᵛ). It in no way resembles the ballad in the letter-book.

nephew should not be shaken either in religion or loyalty by his conversation with Parry'. Anthony certainly was the poorer for the acquaintance, because Dr. Birch found amongst his papers 'a note of Dr. Parry for fifty French crowns borrowed 1 August 1580'. Parry sent some 'intelligence' back to Lord Burleigh.[1]

LVIII. [*No name of addressee*]

Happye ar they that wth good myndes and good meanes bring suche to love and lyve together, whom th opinion of some great and privat injurye hathe set farre a sonder. More happie ar they that, by suche men unto this poynt thus moved, come wyllinglye unto yt. Towarde a parte of this doubled happynesse I wyll, my good cousyn, as an arbitratoure for you as a partie, doo whatsoever I maye. I maye (yf the Lorde so will), about Weddensdaie or Thursdaie in the easter weeke, well attende yt. And thus wth my right hartie comendacons for this tyme I take my leave of you.

From my howse in Saynte Marye Craye, the viij[th] of Marche 1583.

Your assured loving Cousyn

This letter was written on a Sunday, Quadragesima, and Easter in that year fell on 19 April.

LIX. *To the most honorable his verie good Lorde the Erle of Warwicke*

Right sure am I that (my sonne Edwarde Wotton being at the handes of your good Lordeshippe so long a tyme, so many wayes so honorablie used as hee hathe ben), I maye not unto your servaunt Foorde fytlye graunt that that ye requyre mee to doo. Thus standethe the case, the thing that hee desyrethe ys greater then eyther for his welthe hee ys well hable to welde, or for his skyll in husbandrie well instructed to use. And so the thing neyther fyt for hym, nor hee fyt for yt. Besyde this, that person that ys therof nowe my fermoure, ys surelie a verie honest bodye, by

---

[1] Thomas Birch, *Memoirs of Queen Elizabeth*, 1754, vol. i, pp. 12–13.

course in tyme growne to some yeres, and, by the providence of God, become the father of sondrie smale Childerne. And so wolde the removing of hym drawe bothe hym and (as farre as I see), his whole familie to a faire flat beggerye. Whiche thing yf I sholde consent to doo, (as for his interest I might in respecte of Justice yet lawfullye doo), I sholde hardelye wth a merrye mynde passe those fewe daies that the Lorde hathe appoynted mee here to lyve. The weight of whiche poynt I doo in humble sorte referre to the grave consideration of your good Lordeshippe.

And so I beseeche the almightie God in honorable estate to sende you a course of many joyfull yeres. From Pykering howse in London.

LX. *To his verie loving Cousyn Mr Wylforde, servaunt to the right honorable the Lorde Chauncello^r*

Yf the right honorable my verie good Lorde the Lorde Chauncelloure wolde upon my sonne Edwarde Wotton bestowe the office that under hym by his great favoure I nowe have, I sholde accompt mee selfe moche bounde to hym for yt, and be verie gladde of yt. I hope his good Lordeshippe shall fynde hym suche a one as can and will well use yt. Resigne yt, I neede not, nor cannot, having therin none other interest then suche as whollye dependethe upon his good pleasure. This short letter maye geve his good Lordeshippe a sufficient assurance that I am herew^th right well contented, yf for a thing so verelie his owne hee needed yt.

And thus, my good Cousin, with my right hartie comendations for this tyme I take my leave of you.

From my howse in Bocton Malherbe the xth of Auguste 1586.

As no Christian name is given to 'his verie loving Cousyn', it is difficult to identify him. Possibly he was descended from James Wylford, of Hartridge in Cranbrook, midway between Tunbridge Wells and Tenterden, who had died in 1526, leaving a son Thomas, the father of Francis Wylford.[1]

[1] *Archaeologia Cantiana*, vol. lxiii, p. 17, article by Mr. R. H. D'Elboux.

There was also a Thomas Wilforde, of Heden in Kingston, south-east of Canterbury, who was knighted in the Low Countries in 1588, and died in 1611.[1]

The Lord Chancellor was Sir Thomas Bromley. He had held office since 1579, and died in 1587.

---

[1] *Archaeologia Cantiana,* vol. xlviii, p. 31, article by the late Ralph Griffin.

INDEX

PRINTED IN GREAT BRITAIN
AT THE UNIVERSITY PRESS, OXFORD
BY VIVIAN RIDLER
PRINTER TO THE UNIVERSITY